GW01396338

EGYPT:

INTERNAL CHALLENGES

AND REGIONAL STABILITY

CHATHAM HOUSE PAPERS

Chatham House Papers are short monographs on current policy problems which have been commissioned by the Royal Institute of International Affairs. In preparing the paper, authors are advised by a study group of experts convened by the RIIA. Publication of the paper by the Institute indicates its standing as an authoritative contribution to the public debate.

The Royal Institute of International Affairs is an independent body which promotes the rigorous study of international questions and does not express opinions of its own. The opinions expressed in this publication are the responsibility of the authors.

CHATHAM HOUSE PAPERS · 39

EGYPT:

INTERNAL CHALLENGES

AND REGIONAL STABILITY

Edited by Lillian Craig Harris

The Royal Institute of International Affairs

Routledge & Kegan Paul
London, New York and Andover

First published 1988
by Routledge & Kegan Paul Ltd
11 New Fetter Lane, London EC4P 4EE
29 West 35th Street, New York, NY 10001, USA, and
North Way, Andover, Hants SP10 5BE

Reproduced from copy supplied by
Stephen Austin and Sons Ltd and
Printed in Great Britain by
Redwood Burn Limited
Trowbridge, Wiltshire

Library of Congress Cataloging-in-Publication Data

Egypt, internal challenges and regional stability.

    (Chatham House papers ; no. 40)
    "The Royal Institute of International Affairs."
    Bibliography: p.
    Contents: Introduction / Lillian Craig Harris—
Social aspects / Mourad M. Wahba–The economy /
Ali Abdallah—[etc.]
    1. Egypt—Politics and government—1981- .
2. Egypt—Social conditions—1952- . 3. Egypt—
Economic policy. I. Harris, Lillian Craig. II. Royal
Institute of International Affairs. III. Series.
DT107.87.E35   1987   962'.055   87-23525

ISBN 0-7102-1366-2

CONTENTS

ACKNOWLEDGMENTS

This paper is the product of a study group, organized by the Royal Institute of International Affairs, which met regularly for several months during 1987 under the chairmanship of Sir John Moberly, former British ambassador to Iraq and to Jordan. Included in the group were Egyptians, Britons and Americans, who are academics, economists, researchers, journalists and diplomats, both serving and retired.

Financial assistance from the Institute of Energy Economics, in Japan, for which we are most grateful, made possible both the study group and the subsequent publication. The group is also grateful to the Institute's Director of Studies, William Wallace, for administrative support; Pauline Wickham for detailed work on the text; and Nigel Pearce for seeing it through the production process.

Some points of analysis remained controversial within the group, and the opinions expressed in the following chapters should be understood to reflect the conclusions of individual authors only.

August 1987   L.C.H.

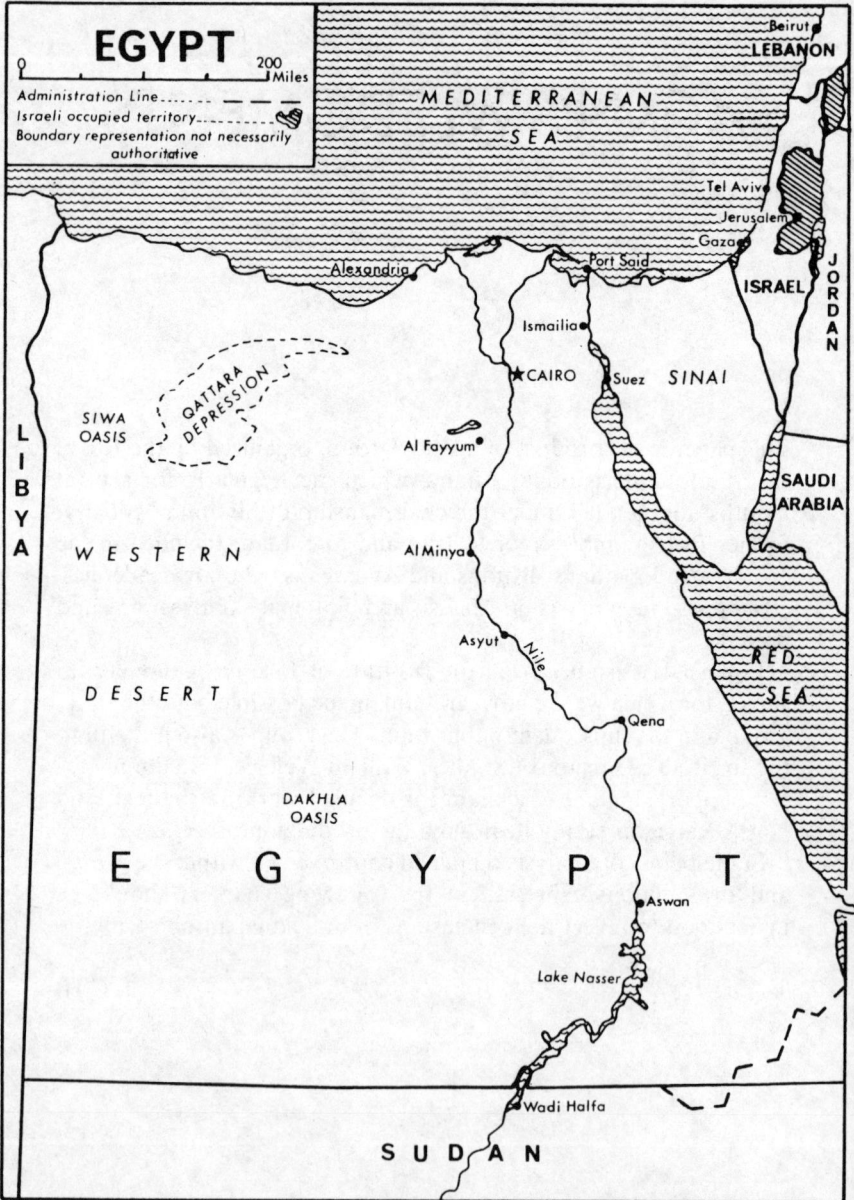

EGYPT

0 _____ 200 Miles

Administration Line ....
Israeli occupied territory ....
Boundary representation not necessarily
authoritative

MEDITERRANEAN SEA

Beirut
LEBANON

Tel Aviv
Jerusalem
Gaza
ISRAEL
JORDAN

Alexandria
Port Said
Ismailia
★ CAIRO
Suez
SINAI

SIWA OASIS

QATTARA DEPRESSION

Al Fayyum

SAUDI ARABIA

LIBYA

WESTERN

Al Minya

Asyut
Nile

RED SEA

DESERT

Qena

DAKHLA OASIS

E G Y P T

Aswan

Lake Nasser

SUDAN

Wadi Halfa

Map Section, L & R Dept., FCO, July 1987

1

INTRODUCTION

Lillian Craig Harris*

Standing, as it does, on the geographic crossroads between Africa, Asia and Europe, Egypt has always excited the imagination of outsiders. Modern Egyptians are a creative *mélange* of Africans and Europeans, Arabs and Nubians, Muslims and Copts, religious devotees and secular pragmatists, peasants and city dwellers. Yet despite centuries of buffeting by outside influences, the Egyptians have managed to maintain their indigenous identity, national integrity and international influence. Their ability to do so has been assisted by geography, the most powerful factor in Egyptian history.

Most of Egypt's approximately one million square kilometres is desert. Only in an area of less than 40,000 square kilometres – about the size of Switzerland – is human habitation normally possible. The source of Egyptian life is, of course, the River Nile, which in its 1,600-kilometre journey from the Sudan to the Mediterranean creates the world's largest oasis. There is almost no rainfall except along the coast, and the country's two-season climate, a relatively cool winter and an extremely hot summer, is marked by dramatic day-to-night variations in temperature, a reminder of the surrounding desert.

*Lillian Craig Harris is the general editor of this volume. A biographical note appears on the back cover.

1

Construction of the High Dam at Aswan in the mid-1960s put an end to the yearly inundations around which Egyptian life had revolved for millennia. Nonetheless, the Nile continues as the regulator of life for, now that it is harnessed in Lake Nasser behind the High Dam, it has increased Egypt's productivity from one yearly crop to three, and expanded permanent habitation in riverine areas. The benefits of the High Dam are among the most visible reminders of the advances in science and technology which have contributed to Egypt's modernization efforts as well as to continuing population growth.

Today there are almost 50 million Egyptians, nearly half of the world's Arabic-speaking peoples. Since 1950, Egypt's population has more than doubled and, with the current annual population growth rate of 2.8% contributing another one million people every 10 months, the population could double again within the next 20 years.

The problems which the Egyptians face are common to many other developing countries: population pressures, limited resources, dependence on international economic assistance, challenges to traditional life-styles, a vociferous but disorganized political opposition. As do other peoples, Egyptians continue to search for means to cope with modernization and the secularization of their lives, and for ways to reaffirm their cultural, religious and political identities.

The main objective of this Chatham House study has been to define Egypt's current problems, social, economic and political, as they relate to both internal and external developments. In considering the relative gravity of Egypt's modern dilemmas, the writers attempt contemporary answers to the age-old question, 'Is Egypt running out of time?'

The social situation
Egyptian social structure relies on firmly held religious values and strong family ties. With its emphasis on the fulfilment of one's designated social role, rather than on the development of individual talent or the satisfaction of personal goals and desires, Egyptian culture is geared to the welfare of the group, the family in particular. Values such as the central importance of the family and the primacy of male authority remain extremely strong, and the country's overall

low crime rate reflects the strength of a social system which stresses group responsibility, honour and traditional virtues.

A group-oriented society of this kind does not adjust easily to change. Today many Egyptians feel threatened by challenges to the old social order, particularly evident in the changing role of women and young people as a result of modernization and of urbanization and subsequent overcrowding. Government efforts to control population growth are frequently rejected as intrusive, damaging to family economics and against God's will. Proponents of population control are sometimes countered with the argument that Egypt's path to economic recovery is not a family, but a government, responsibility, which must be met through the creation of more jobs.

Nearly half of all Egyptians live in the country's two major cities, Cairo and Alexandria, where the square footage of living space and quality of accommodation continue to deteriorate and unemployment proliferates. Even those rural migrants fortunate enough to obtain reasonable employment in the city often find that the quality of their lives has declined. The highly stratified social structure of the village has disappeared, family and group ties have weakened, women find themselves with new contacts and responsibilities outside the home, children move into educational and social spheres not understood or approved by their parents.

In both urban and rural Egypt, population growth moves ahead of the government's ability to provide adequate health, education and social benefits, and often ahead of family hopes of providing for children at least the quality of life available to their parents. Millions live in poverty, malnourishment is frequent though hunger is not, and the infant mortality rate remains high. Hospitals and other social services are under tremendous strain and often function inadequately.

International aid is assisting in construction of a new sewerage system and an underground transit system to alleviate pressures on Cairo's antiquated and overextended sanitation and transportation networks. Ambitious though these projects are, it remains obscure how far such efforts will succeed in eliminating the massive traffic jams, air pollution and water and sewerage problems of a still expanding city whose basic utilities were designed to cope with the demands of no more than two million people. Inadequate maintenance, even of new facilities, remains a serious deficiency.

More serious for Egypt's future, the quality of education received in most of the country's schools and universities has deteriorated sharply since 1970, largely because of overcrowding. Although about two-thirds of Egypt's children attend school for most of the nine years of compulsory education, overcrowded and inadequate facilities continue to lessen the value of time spent in school. Despite the universal availability of education since the 1952 revolution, 50% of Egyptians remain illiterate and among women the figure may be as high as 75%.

Lack of employment opportunities and low salaries at home continue to lure the cream of each year's graduates to jobs abroad. For those who stay, even 'guaranteed' government jobs may take months or even years to acquire, and housing shortages seriously restrict prospects for employment and marriage. There is, moreover, a rising discrepancy between the abysmally low salaries of the several million civil servants and the larger sums commanded by business personnel and even by semi-skilled workers. Underemployment in Egypt's unwieldy and overstaffed bureaucracy is another source of unhappiness, as is inflation, which has cut deep into the benefits provided by the government pension system.

In such conditions, many take traditional refuge in God, seeking relief in religion from the hardships of life and from the spiritual emptiness which often characterizes the lives of the disadvantaged and displaced. Most Egyptians are opposed to the use of religion as a servant of party politics, but because religion and state are theoretically indivisible in Islam, religion retains a potent role as the justifier of political action. Former President Sadat, for example, found it politically advantageous to obtain a *fatwa* (religious decree) from the *'ulama* (learned religious authorities) of Al-Azhar legitimizing the 1979 Egyptian peace treaty with Israel. Moreover, because they see in religion an answer to all of life's problems, a sizeable body of Egyptians from all walks of life continue their efforts to move the government to apply an exclusively Islamic legal code (*shari'a*).

Nor has modern Egypt ever been without those who advocate violence as the path to political transformation. Islamic extremists murdered Sadat in 1981, and militant religious groups remain the subject of careful government surveillance. Although such radicals operate mainly underground and the number of their members and sympathizers is unknown, their attractiveness in a deteriorating social and economic environment is self-evident. Particularly vulnerable are the malcontented urban poor and the university students, who fear that the promised benefits of education will be denied to them by Egypt's beleaguered society.

Historically the Egyptians have not been easily stirred to violence. But when their honour is impugned or when economic circumstances sink below acceptance levels, they can demonstrate their anger with great violence and determination. Today many Egyptians are concerned over the prospects for violence created by the country's mounting social and economic difficulties. Moreover, the aspirations and activities of Muslim radicals are deeply frightening to their fellow citizens, Muslim as well as Coptic. The canker of sectarian violence waits just beneath the skin of Egyptian society, periodically erupting in ugly incidents.

Chapter 2, which deals with these social aspects of Egyptian life, focuses in particular on the implications of population expansion, and examines social alienation and the threat of sectarian violence in the light of declining social services, growing inequalities in income distribution and increased unemployment.

The economic situation

During the past 150 years, Egypt has frequently been on the edge of economic ruin. Although a desire for economic reform played a major role in the 1952 revolution, since then the government has remained unable to set a clear economic course. In brief, Nasser turned Egypt towards socialism and the Soviet bloc to achieve both military and civil development, and made vigorous efforts, including extensive land reform and the decimation of the entrepreneurial class, to eliminate inequalities in the distribution of wealth. The government became increasingly involved in the economy, and by the mid-1960s had assumed control of the financial, communications and utilities infrastructures, as well as of a large part of the manufacturing and construction industries, foreign trade and the transportation systems.

Westerners generally attribute Egypt's current economic woes to the excesses of the Nasser period. For many Egyptians, on the other hand, the 1960s represent a golden age of low prices. Sadat's assumption of the presidency in 1970 brought measures to reverse the policies of socialism and to introduce *infitah,* or an 'open door' policy of international economic integration. But subsequent policies have not solved the country's problems. Although President Mubarak has expanded upon Sadat's encouragement of private investment in the Egyptian economy, the early promise of *infitah* has not been realized. Instead, there has been growing dependence on international aid, and on that of the United States in particular.

Since 1984, the Egyptian economy has been stagnant. During 1987 Egypt's four chief sources of foreign exchange and revenue – petroleum, tourism, the Suez Canal, and remittances from Egyptian workers abroad – continued at levels lower than those of the early 1980s. The most immediate problems are a sizeable budget and balance-of-payments deficit, a serious shortage of foreign exchange and a large external debt burden. Conditions for continued assistance from both the International Monetary Fund and the World Bank include a commitment by the Egyptian government to far-reaching economic reforms, including the removal, or at least reduction, of enormous government subsidies on utilities, transportation and basic food commodities.

But reform is an explosive political issue. For millions of Egyptians near or below the poverty line, virtually any tampering with government assistance programmes is a threat to survival. Serious rioting occurred over cuts to bread subsidies in 1977, and the prospect of a return to such unrest is frequently cited by government authorities as a reason for caution in economic reform policies.

Chapter 3, in looking at these economic issues, pays special attention to the components of Egypt's present economic crisis in the light of the recent past and discusses measures necessary to reverse the economic decline. Both fundamental and immediate problems are discussed, as is the outlook for the future.

Internal political scene
Since coming to office on the death of Sadat in 1981, President Hosni Mubarak has sought to avoid the pharaonic style of both Nasser and Sadat. By European standards, Mubarak wields tremendous personal authority and on several occasions has extended the State of Emergency instituted by Sadat to provide the government with extraordinary powers. But Mubarak is not a personally popular president and, judged against the Egyptian ideal of leader as father figure, is frequently criticized for lack of initiative and forcefulness.

There are widespread complaints that even after six years in office Mubarak 'has not proved himself'.

Nonetheless, although Mubarak has not solved the country's economic crisis, Egyptians admit that he has lessened the constraints on political opposition by allowing greater freedom to the political opponents of the ruling National Democratic Party. Five opposition parties have now been given legal status, and the influence of the opposition is growing. During Mubarak's tenure, political prisoners have been released and sectarian tensions reduced. And no one accuses the president of the corruption for which Sadat's regime has been castigated. Egyptians also point with pride to Mubarak's efforts to return Egypt to a position of more active international leadership.

President Mubarak's priorities seem straightforward. He has sought to provide greater freedom of public expression, to maintain internal security, to restore Egypt's standing in the Arab world while retaining the peace treaty with Israel, and to work towards the eventual solution of economic problems, including narrowing the gap between rich and poor and cracking down on corruption. In a speech in April 1987, he described the 'predominant features' of his time in office as 'democracy, development, security and purity as evidenced in our actions'.[1]

Mubarak's task is complicated by a multitude of factors, including the stagnant economy, an enormous and dysfunctional government bureaucracy, popular resistance to government austerity measures, and popular disillusionment with the political process. Though Egyptians are intensely interested in politics, the country suffers from a general lethargy as regards political involvement. Only some 25% of voters participated in the April 1987 parliamentary elections although voting is a duty required by law. Typically, while Egyptians will make vociferous demands that 'something must be done', many retain the cynical view that those in authority have already decided what to do and therefore even to vote is a waste of time.

Unlike Sadat, Mubarak has not appointed a vice-president, a position that would be seen to indicate a successor designate. Alternatives to Mubarak's leadership remain difficult to identify. That all three Egyptian presidents have been military men reflects, as some see it, a strong national predilection for military leadership. Other observers counter that this phenomenon reflects the Egyptian military's propensity to take the initiative in times of crisis. Some knowledgeable Egyptians claim, however, that their country is ready for a change from military leadership: Mubarak himself has sought to lower the numbers of active military personnel in government positions. Nonetheless, the Egyptian military remains the ultimate guarantor of political power and will continue to play a critical role in any power transfer.

Chapter 4, 'Domestic politics', concentrates on the evolution of Egypt's political system, the factors which weigh for and against political liberalization, and the prospects for continuity and change.

External factors
Egypt considers itself a member of both the Arab and the African worlds and exercises considerable influence and leadership in both spheres as well as in the Third World more generally. It is a founding member of both the Non-Aligned Movement and the Organization of African Unity, and finds additional incentive for friendly ties with its southern neighbours in its concern over the potential of the black African states to obstruct the waters of the Nile. Special ties with the Sudan reflect close economic and historical relationships. Mubarak's regime has succeeded in strengthening Egypt's ties with the West while reducing the tensions of the Sadat era with the Soviet Union, has increased trade with a variety of countries, has sought to reassert Egypt's role as an African leader and has secured financial assistance or relief for the country from a variety of international sources.

Most Arab states broke off diplomatic relations with Egypt following the Egypt-Israel peace treaty. (Oman and the Sudan retained diplomatic ties, and Jordan re-established ties in 1985.) Nonetheless, conventional wisdom holds that owing to Egypt's influence with the West and recognized leadership position, the Arab world needs Egypt more than Egypt needs the Arab world. Certainly, Egypt's influence was such that, outside the political sphere, relations with the Arabs continued much as usual. Although Egypt has not rejoined the Arab League following its expulsion in 1979 for signing the peace treaty with Israel, in 1984 it was readmitted to the Organization of the Islamic Conference. More recently, some of the Gulf states have reinstituted financial aid. And, at the early 1987 Islamic summit, Egypt was informally welcomed back into the Arab fold.

The government of Egypt claims continued commitment to its peace treaty with Israel despite significant popular dissatisfaction with that treaty. (There is widespread unease at the continuation of diplomatic relations with Israel, but no impetus for a return to overt hostilities.) Although some trade and technical cooperation has developed between the two countries, relations remain mutually suspicious. Outstanding problems include an ownership dispute over the small Sinai enclave of Taba, and Israeli treatment of Palestinians in the occupied territories and actions in Lebanon. Concerted Egyptian efforts in the 1980s to move the Arab/Israel peace process forward by serving as a broker among the parties to the conflict have so far been unsuccessful.

Egypt prides itself on non-alignment and has strong economic and political ties with both the United States and the Soviet Union. However, as both the Egyptian economy and the Egyptian military establishment have become increasingly dependent on American assistance, Mubarak's image has been tarnished by public perception of him as an American client. (After Israel, Egypt is the world's largest recipient of American economic and military assistance.) On several occasions, Mubarak has been deeply embarrassed, in view of his close American connection, by his inability to redirect US policy in the Middle East.

In an effort to diversify sources of aid and technology, and to increase Egypt's international political leverage, Mubarak has worked to strengthen Egypt's ties with the European Community as well as with Eastern Europe. Such efforts have borne fruit in financial assistance and commercial agreements. The EC's call in February and July 1987 for an international peace conference on the Middle East parallels Egyptian efforts to move the peace process forward.

Chapter 5, Egypt's external relations, speculates on the future of Egypt's regional and international roles and examines the prospects for a radical change in its pro-Western alignment.

Ever since Muhammad Ali Pasha led Egypt into the modern era during the early nineteenth century, Westerners have not ceased to provide advice on how to 'fix' Egypt's problems. Although much of this advice has been good, some of it has been contradictory, some impracticable, some unreasonable and the bulk of it rejected. Nonetheless, Egypt's position as a crossroads between continents and cultures dictates that its future will remain of consequence and interest far beyond its borders.

Notes
1 BBC, *Summary of World Broadcasts*, Middle East and Africa, 6 April 1987, A/10.

2

SOCIAL ASPECTS

Mourad M. Wahba*

Thirty-five years after the 1952 coup, Egypt is once more on the boil. There is a generalized, confused feeling in society, a sense that the identity of state and population achieved under Nasser has been lost. The signs of the alienation which led to the instability of the late 1940s and early 1950s, and eventually to the military takeover, have reappeared. It is the purpose of this paper to examine the manifestations of Egypt's ills during the first half of the 1980s, linking these ills to the increased alienation of the greater part of the people from the mechanisms as well as the ideals of the political process, and speculating upon the political repercussions of this alienation.

Historical background
When the Free Officers came to power in July 1952, they found a society which was to a very large extent discontented with its government. A 'democratic' parliament elected by a largely illiterate rural population discussed the social ills of society and timorously recommended changes in the social order, but was clearly incapable of implementing these changes. These social ills were defined by a then popular slogan as 'poverty, ignorance and disease'. They were, according to the Free Officers, endemic in Egyptian society, and

*Mourad M. Wahba teaches at the American University, Cairo.

their remedy lay far beyond the powers of an impotent parliament dominated by rural notables, a government of semi-feudal land-owners, or the tycoons of commerce and industry. The powerless-ness of the government before 1952 led to such expressions of alienation as widespread industrial unrest and *jacqueries* in the countryside resulting in the brief and bloody occupation of large estates by the peasants working on them.

The politically active population in the towns tended to gather under four main banners: those of the Communist Party, the Muslim Brotherhood, the Young Egypt Party and the Wafd Party. The Communists, led by the Democratic Movement for National Liberation (better known by its Arabic acronym Hadeto), had the support of some students and some intellectuals, as well as of a small but growing number of factory workers and craftsmen. The Muslim Brotherhood, which had started outside Cairo, in the Canal Zone in 1928, succeeded in garnering the support of the more traditional youth. It based its programme on a call for national independence and the setting up of an Islamic system of government, and soon saw its influence and membership spread to the capital and the rest of Egypt. The third group, the crypto-fascist Young Egypt Party, renamed the Socialist Party after World War II, also concentrated on social ills and sought to influence political life through the formation of its own militia. Finally, the old nationalist party, the Wafd, which had deserted the streets for Parliament after the nationalist demonstrations of 1919, had become embittered by three decades of nationalist struggle and returned once more to mass politics. Its social programme was enlarged to include limited social security proposals, the leadership of student demonstrations against the British occupation, and the formation of its own militia.

Despite the differences between these groups, they shared three important characteristics. The first of these was their willingness to act outside the traditional channels of Parliament, as demonstrated in the 1952 burning of Cairo,* and by the formation of more or less violent militias as their 'active wings'. Political programmes and demands were expressed mainly through demonstrations, and the relatively free press. A second characteristic was the increasing

---

*The arson started in the central business district, and was attributed by some to the Brotherhood and by others to the secret police. The identity of the perpetrators, however, was never established with any degree of certainty.

concentration of the political programmes of these parties on demands for social remedies to the ills of 'poverty, ignorance and disease'. Last came their preoccupation with the goal of national independence, and an increasing distrust of the elected government's ability to achieve this aim. After the 1942 encircling of the King's palace by British tanks and the humiliating defeat of 1948 in Palestine, the government was regarded with a large degree of contempt. The first event was seen as the King capitulating to British demands for the formation of a Wafdist government against his express wishes; the second brought home the state of corruption and disorganization in the army which led to the defeat of the largest army in the region by the forces of a fledgling Israel.

Until the defeat of 1948, the army largely stood outside the political process. An indication of this collective indifference is the fact that when the future Free Officers first entered the political fray, it was as members of *civilian* political movements, and they often shifted their allegiance, without apparent reason, from one grouping to the next. The Free Officers did, in fact, have many traits in common with civil society, such as dissatisfaction with current political institutions and a belief in national independence and the necessity for social reform. The general state of unrest in Egyptian society up to 1952, the separation of the mass of the people from the parliamentary process, the generalized feeling of an inability to identify with an impotent, humiliated government and the confused expressions of a desire for change – all these indicated the degree of alienation prevailing in society at the time. Nasser himself likened this state of affairs to that in Pirandello's *Six Characters in Search of an Author*, a play he greatly admired.

The policies of the Free Officers, after taking power, were designed to a large extent to meet these problems of Egyptian society in the late 1940s and early 1950s. They managed to achieve national independence, and implemented measures to relieve the social ills of poverty, disease and ignorance. They also acted outside the framework of traditional political institutions, trying first to start national mass movements based upon a condensation of the various political programmes of the 1940s, and then settling for a single-party system.

The measures taken after 1952 comprised an ambitious programme for social reform, including the confiscation and redistribution of large estates, the setting up of rural centres for health care, the electrification of the countryside, free access to education for the masses and an encouragement of social mobility. The other main contribution was the speeding up of the trend towards industrialization and away from a dependence upon agriculture, and specifically cotton, as the main source of income. There was also a marked resort to extra-parliamentary action, such as rule by presidential decree, and the subversion of 'bourgeois' parliamentary action by means of a regulation claiming half the seats in Parliament for 'workers and peasants', however loosely defined. The power of the press was recognized, with the young government taking control of newspapers and magazines and putting Free Officers in charge of new or nationalized press empires. The result was a form of populism – 'Nasserism' – which had much in common with the populist regimes in the newly independent Third World and Latin America.

Today, despite the promise and aspirations of the 1952 coup, Egypt again faces a number of crises. The first of these is the growth in population, seen by many observers as the *fons et origo* of Egypt's social ills. The second relates to the breakdown of the social welfare system in the 1950s and 1960s. The third problem, resulting from the second, represents the various attempts of the population to come to terms with a system which it feels can no longer deliver its part of the implicit social contract struck in the aftermath of World War II: a welfare state providing employment, education and health care.

Is population a key problem?

The title of this section would at first appear to pose a redundant question. According to a highly alarmist report of the Central Agency for Public Mobilization and Statistics (CAPMAS) in 1985, Egypt's population increases by one person every 24.4 seconds, or by 1.294 million a year.[1] The population should therefore have reached the 50-million mark by the middle of 1986. If the rate of growth continues to be 2.8%, CAPMAS estimates that the population will reach 68 million by the year 2000, with Greater Cairo alone accounting for 15 million persons. Given that 4% of the total area of Egypt is inhabitable (the rest being inhospitable deserts), population density in Egypt is very high, although subject to great variability. For instance, the population density in Cairo varies from 7.7

thousand per square kilometre in the middle- and upper-class district of Kasr el-Nil to 118 thousand in the lower-class districts of Bab-el-Shaaria and Rod-el-Faraq, the last two of which, incidentally, have been centres for the resurgence of Islamic fundamentalism during the past decade.

The most densely populated area of Egypt, however, is not in Cairo but in Alexandria; this is the harbour district of al-Gumruk, where some 156,000 persons are packed in every square kilometre. Taken together, Cairo and Alexandria account for a quarter of the population of Egypt and more than half the urban population. Indeed, the population of Egypt is now divided roughly equally between rural and urban areas, with the urban rate of growth outstripping that of the rural areas. Thus, the average rate of growth in urban conglomerations over the past fifty years has been around 4.5% per annum, of which only 1.5% is accounted for by the rate of rural-urban migration.[2] Such statistics give the lie to the popular myth in Egypt that population growth is mainly due to ignorant peasants lacking alternative means of distraction.

The high rate of population growth has been seen by Egyptians as well as by international aid agencies as Egypt's main problem. Is it, however, the key problem in understanding Egypt's recent failures, or in unlocking the door to future growth? It appears too late, in 1987, to influence the rate of growth in time to effect any major changes by the year 2000. Were this possible, the reduction of the average number of children from 5.4 to 3 per family would result only in the equivalent of a GDP per capita increase of 0.7% per annum after some 23 years.[3] The efforts of a family planning campaign, begun in 1966, have resulted in a negligible decrease in population growth of 0.04% in recent years, whereas the government plan calls for a 0.1% decrease each year.[4]

The causes of the large growth in Egypt's population have been documented over the years. These are the reduction in infant mortality and increased life expectancy because of improvements in health; the need for quasi-free labour in the fields as a result of recent migration to the towns and abroad, which has depleted manpower in villages; and the perception that a large number of children is an insurance policy against old age and poverty. In addition, religious factors have contributed to the failure of the family planning programme.

Thus, on the Muslim side, contraception is seen as a sin; the Azhar *fatwa** required to legitimize contraception has not been forthcoming. Moreover, a variety of popular preachers, local Savonarolas, hurl fiery invective against the ungodly who would refuse the grace of a child. On the Coptic side, there is a conscious effort to increase the number of children in order to redress, in the only way possible, the population imbalance which has resulted in Copts, Egypt's Christians, perceiving themselves as a beleaguered minority.

Official campaigns for family planning, ranging from the insultingly patronizing to the frankly panicky, have been largely unsuccessful. One television campaign presents an animated film of two peasants, Hassanein and Muhammedein, speaking with a ham Upper Egyptian accent, one of whom defeats the other in a mock duel – the implication being that the victor has fewer children. This presumably is aimed at the rural population, although the effectiveness of mocking people as a method of controlling population growth would appear dubious. The second campaign, also televised, but very much in evidence on posters in Cairo and Alexandria, is the *Unzur Hawlak* (Look Around) campaign. In this effort, a poor urban family is shown surrounded by hosts of children who are all yelling at once while dragging their unfortunate parents into poverty. The targets of these campaigns are always the poorest strata of the population, for whom inadequate standards of hygiene lead to a high rate of infant mortality. However, these are not the only groups pushing up the rate of population growth. Craftsmen and traders seeking to achieve the kudos of a male heir to their newfound fortune can afford to have many children as a mirror of their wealth, rather than as a source of income.

The family planning campaign rests upon the Malthusian presupposition that Egypt has reached bursting point so far as population is concerned; that the 4% inhabitable area is already too densely populated; and that the country's resources cannot be stretched to accommodate more people. This is certainly true of the currently inhabited area of the country, but the possibility of increasing the size of provincial towns which already exist, as well as the creation of satellite towns in the desert, has not yet been fully explored.

---

*An opinion on matters of religious law delivered by the theological authorities at the al-Azhar mosque.

Moreover, a large population is and has been a source of labour, exportable to neighbouring labour-poor countries and employable in the event of Egypt's industrial base growing. In addition, as shown by the Southeast Asian economies, a large population base can serve as a large domestic market and therefore help in the economic development of the country. Finally, the large population is not the sole source of Egypt's economic problems. Foreign debt is an important factor, a quarter of which is attributable to the import of weapons, not grain, and another sizeable proportion to the import of consumer luxuries such as motorcars.

This does not detract from the fact that Egypt's population will have increased by some 20 million in the year 2000. It should be emphasized, however, that the present growth rate is not particularly high for the Third World in general: the average rate of population growth for Africa, for instance, stands at 3%, while that for the Arab world is 3.4%. Nevertheless, a rapidly expanding population does impose strains on development efforts and on the country's infrastructure. These strains may lead to the problems of overpopulation in the future, when the population level has reached a point at which it is no longer a development asset. It is therefore important to ensure the cheap, plentiful availability of means of contraception for those who wish to make use of them.

More importantly, as long as the causes of the high increase in population are not tackled through a comprehensive development policy, no amount of government propaganda will induce people to stop having children. A reduction of the population growth can be effected through an increase in literacy and education. In addition, increasing economic difficulties already make it difficult for young couples to afford to marry and find suitable housing. The current economic crisis has also resulted in an ever-growing number of marriages in which both partners have to work outside the home. All these factors are instrumental in controlling levels of population growth.

To conclude, the high rate of population growth is a serious problem only because of its emotiveness as an issue and because of congestion in the towns. Urban overcrowding is not a problem of population growth so much as of deficient urban planning. It is possible, however, to envisage a time when overpopulation does become a serious problem. The current government campaign, for a variety of reasons, has failed to reach its targeted audience. A radical

17

reappraisal of the economic and social reasons for population growth is therefore vital before an appropriate and effective strategy can be devised to deal with it.

The decline of the welfare state

As already noted, one of the main bases for the legitimacy of the post-1952 regime was the creation of the welfare state. In this section, I would like to argue that the welfare state has declined in the last decade. This can be seen in the provision and conditions of employment, a lowering in the standards of education and health, and a worsening of income distribution.

Employment

The distribution of Egypt's population has radically changed over the last century. Whereas in 1907 some 82% of its people lived in rural areas, this figure had declined to 56% in the 1976 census. Already, population projections based upon an extrapolation of preceding trends suggest that, for the first time in Egyptian history, the majority of the population now lives in urban centres.[5] Similarly, the labour force has become largely urbanized, so that by 1976 the share of agriculture in the provision of employment had dropped to 42%, before declining rapidly to 34.6% for 1984–5. Indeed, by the year 1986–7, the Five-Year Plan (1982–7) predicted a decrease in the share of the labour force employed in agriculture to 34%.[6]

Urban sector employment has increased *pari passu* with the urban population. Most of the increase, following the customary pattern in the Third World, has been in the service sector, where employment in public utilities and other services (the bulk of which represents employment in the government) rose from 23.6% of the labour force in 1976 to 30% in 1984.[7] Not all the increase in service sector employment, however, ought to be attributed to urban concentration, for there is also a slow but steady growth in rural services employing, for example, cooperative employees, irrigation engineers, health service personnel, and government staff and engineers to service the increasing mechanization of agricultural implements.

There are further imbalances in the labour market. A high dependency ratio means that every member of the population in the working age-group (12–65) has to support three others. This statistic, however, does not take into account the relatively high rate of unemployment in society, which is obviously more important in the case of women working outside the home, who form only 7% of the labour force (although most women in rural areas work in some capacity in the fields). Much has been made, in literature on Egypt, of the persistence of Nasserist policies of guaranteed state employment for graduates and army leavers. Recent evidence suggests, however, that even if these policies have not been officially abandoned, they are implemented with a high degree of laxity. Thus, by mid-1987, not all university graduates for the year 1981 had been found government employment, and in technical institutes those who had graduated in 1980 were still waiting for appointments. Indeed, after delays amounting on average to four or five years, only 25,000–30,000 graduates of universities and technical institutes out of an average annual number of 120,000 are given a job in the government or public sector.[8]

Unemployment, according to official figures, is around 5% of the labour force. This is not borne out by other figures. Thus, the 1976 census showed that some 56% of the population of 15 years old and over was not employed: i.e. 10 million. If we restrict our analysis to the male labour force, the percentage of those defined by the census as 'not occupied' is 19.2%. Subtract 3.5% of that number over the age of 65, and we reach the conclusion that 16% of the male population between the ages of 15 and 65 is 'not occupied'. In addition, those who are occupied are not always gainfully so. Thus, one report states that in agriculture there are some 200 days worked on average every year, while Ayubi argues that at least a third of the country's bureaucracy is redundant.[9]

The problem of employment, however, appears to be one of market segmentation rather than one of non-existence of jobs. Some sectors of the labour market are in dire need of labour, such as the agricultural sector at certain times of the year and the construction sector, where an estimated 40% of the work force has migrated in search of high salaries in the oil-rich Arab states of the region. This has led to the distressing phenomenon of child labour on a large scale. UNICEF statistics estimate the number of children working in Egypt to be around the 2-million mark. Ninety per cent of these children are between the ages of 6 and 12, in blatant contravention of the country's labour laws. The majority are employed in the agricultural and construction sectors to replace migrant adult labour, and perform light jobs in ice-making factories, cotton-carding, carpet-weaving and repair workshops, where their health is often impaired. A World Health Organization report states that 70% of children thus employed are open to work-related infections, including lung and eye diseases. In addition, a large number of children are employed to perform menial jobs in the city, such as shoe-shining, garbage collection and petty trade.[10]

Education

The provision of free education was achieved by a Wafdist government in the 1940s at the instigation of the writer (and, later, Minister of Education) Taha Hussein. It was expanded by subsequent governments under the Free Officers, and has been a decisive element in making possible the large degree of social mobility in the country since 1952. Despite the increase in numbers, however, the quality of education has deteriorated. This can be seen in the increase in the average number of children per classroom from 39.3 in 1982–3 to 42.1 in 1986–7. Moreover, despite primary education being free and compulsory, the UNICEF study referred to above indicates that 32% of children of school age will leave school before having completed their primary studies. Twenty per cent of the remaining children are regularly absent from school in order to work. As a result, it is estimated that 40% of children who have had primary education, or 22% of Egypt's population, revert to illiteracy.[11] Indeed, some observers have estimated Egypt's illiteracy rate to be nearer 60%–65%.

University education has followed the trend set by primary education. There has been an increase in the number of universities in Egypt, which now number twelve, in addition to the private American University in Cairo. These are the universities of Cairo, Ain Shams and al-Azhar, Alexandria, Assiut, Tanta, Mansoura, Zagazig, Helwan, the Suez Canal, Minia and Menufia. The cumulative number of students enrolled in these universities reached 682,348 in 1984–5. Of this number, more than three-quarters, 513,905, were enrolled in the humanities, while the remainder went to the faculties of medicine, dentistry and pharmacology, engineering, agriculture, sciences, technology, veterinary medicine and nursing, and 'reconstruction planning'. The medical faculties and engineering, taken together, account for 76,000 students, nearly half the enrolment outside the humanities.[12] The level of education in these faculties is inadequate, with overcrowded lecture halls, where up to a thousand students are subject to the perorations of a professor whose assistants then repeat the lessons to smaller groups. Emphasis is on memory, libraries are poorly stocked, and students who can afford it must buy mimeographed course notes or take private lessons (paid for in dollars in some faculties, such as medicine and engineering) in order to obtain a degree.

Health

Despite the progress made by the government in opening rural health centres, and the increase in life expectancy, the picture on the health side of social services is not all positive. Thus, whereas there were 1.97 hospital beds for every 1,000 persons in 1981–2, there were only 1.8 in 1986–7.[13] This figure, however, does not take into account the number of hospital beds in private hospitals which have been opened in the past ten years. Private hospitals are too expensive, though, for the majority of the population, costing as much as the monthly salary of a middle-level bureaucrat for a day's stay, not including the medical treatment.

On a more general level, there has been an increase in some endemic diseases despite attempts to control them. For instance, the increase, after the construction of the Aswan High Dam, in the area of fields irrigated through a perennial irrigation system (rather than the old basin system) has led to an increase in the spread of bilharzia. Infection with bilharzia thus affects around 46% of the population, i.e. most of the rural population of Egypt. This disease, spread by a parasite, leads to the general debilitation of those affected by it, and sometimes to their death. The most important effect, however, of the change in the irrigation system has been the spread of the disease to Lower Egypt, where it was extremely rare in the past. In 1982 the highest levels of infection were in Beheira Governorate (62%), and the lowest levels were in Menufia (25%). [14]

In addition, a report to the President of the Republic presented in 1986 emphasized the detrimental effects of a growing addiction to drugs in society, notably hashish, but also commercial preparations such as amphetamines. There are also reports of the reintroduction of heroin – a drug which had not been used in Egypt for nearly thirty years. The use of the more expensive drugs is not confined to the gilded youth of the country, but is found increasingly among craftsmen, whose dramatic rise in income since the mid-1970s makes these drugs affordable. In contrast, the use of hashish has spread mainly to rural areas, with adverse effects on health and consequently productivity.[15] Finally, account should be taken of the deleterious effect of substantial resources being channelled into the black economy through the production and distribution of narcotics.

Income distribution
It is in the light of the figures on employment and social welfare that income distribution data should be viewed. Information on income distribution and levels of poverty is not regularly collected by the governmental statistical agency (CAPMAS) and is perforce sketchy. What we do know, however, is that wages as a proportion of GDP had reached the high level of 50% in 1970. This share had decreased to 37.9% in 1983–4. Moreover, the 1976 census indicated that whereas the richest 10% of the population received slightly more than a third of national income, the poorest 60% also received a third. The percentage of urban families under a poverty line of £E351 rose from 34% to 38% during the period after 1974–5. This proportion rose to 44%, using a poverty line of £E270, in the case of rural families.[16] These figures, however, should not be taken as being wholly accurate, since an increasing number of people, especially in urban areas, take on a variety of jobs to supplement their declared incomes.

Coping with alienation
The developments reviewed in the preceding pages have had many effects upon Egyptian society. Migration to the cities has alienated the majority of the population, of rural origin, from their stable existence. In addition, the deterioration of social services and the inefficiency of the welfare state, which became most visible during the 1970s and 1980s, has led to a loss of trust in the government as 'providence'. Students and army leavers have seen their expectations of sinecures in the bureaucracy come to nought, poverty has probably increased in the countryside, and the standard of living in the cities has deteriorated for the majority of the population. It is estimated that one million people live in the graveyards of Cairo for want of housing. Against this backdrop of increasing misery, there is the offensive wealth of a new class of master-craftsmen, traders,

contractors and businessmen – not all of whom are noted for their scrupulous honesty – who display their newly acquired luxuries in the crowded streets of Cairo and Alexandria.

The response of the majority of the population has been a sense of alienation, or even feelings of revolt at the injustice of a society which had based its legitimacy upon 'Sufficiency and Justice', according to the Nasserist slogan. The bread riots of 18 and 19 January 1977 and the February 1986 mutiny of conscripts in the security forces are indications of the strength of such feelings. In both these cases, the targets for the rioters' incendiary ire and desperate looting were the symbols of injustice: the night-clubs on the Pyramids Road, luxury hotels and private motor-cars. There have been, however, more muted expressions of this alienation and revolt against social injustice: namely, the migration to the oil-rich Arab states in pursuit of higher income, the return to greater religious commitment and the search for the City of God.

The precise number of Egyptians employed in neighbouring Arab countries is not known. For one thing, most Arab countries, for obvious domestic political reasons, do not publish statistics on the number of foreigners they employ. For another, although the Egyptian government, mainly for fiscal purposes, does try to find out the number of Egyptians employed abroad, there are many who migrate in search of higher incomes without declaring their status to the authorities. Estimates of Egyptian labour abroad varied in 1984 between an unofficial figure of 2.2–2.5 million workers (with one million in Iraq alone) and the figure of 1.574 million provided by the Egyptian Ministry of Labour.[17]

Most Egyptians who migrate do so for specific reasons rather than as a general indication of their displeasure with the political or social situation. Villagers, for instance, will take an illegal and highly dangerous caravan route to Libya in order to find work which will finance a specific project, such as marriage, or buying an electric pump or tractor, or building a stone house, or even purchasing their own plot of land. In the cities, the main reason for migration appears to be financing the purchase of a flat in order to get married, or in order that one's children might get married. Thus the aim of the migrant labourer, whether in the city or in the countryside, is to find the means to finance part of his or her welfare which the state has been unable to provide.

The other form of migration is internal. This is the migration – or withdrawal from society – referred to in the name of the extremist group al-Takfir w'al Hijra (Excommunication and Emigration). Active political involvement in the extreme Islamic movements tends to be concentrated in the cities, among the educated youth and university students. It is these groups that came to rely most on the welfare state and promises of social mobility. Such promises were to a large extent frustrated, and replaced instead by the infuriating spectacle of the New Rich parading their wealth.

The dream of national independence, which formed part of the legitimating discourse of the Nasserist state, and which was fed to all schoolchildren throughout their education, was shattered by the 1967 defeat in the Six-Day War, by a peace seen as humiliating and by the clear domination of foreigners in the national economy as well as the polity. (Witness the negative popular reaction over the hijacking of the Egyptair plane by US forces in 1985.) This perception of being dominated by foreigners is evident not only in the ideological discourse of Muslim fundamentalist extremists, who draw upon a tradition of popular religious leaders leading the revolt against perceived excesses of authority and injustice, but also in popular reactions to events that are seen as national humiliations.

After the mysterious death of Soliman Khater, the private who was jailed for shooting Israeli tourists in the Sinai in 1985, there were demonstrations with slogans against 'the Jews and the Crusaders'. (The Jews, of course are a code name for Israel, and the Crusaders for the West, i.e. foreign Christians. Local Christian communities, when they are attacked, are referred to as Nazarenes.) Demonstrators on this and other occasions were not all members of extreme Islamic organizations, a fact which indicates the extent to which the discourse of these organizations has become commonplace.

In the face of increasing alienation from a society which held so much promise yet led to such disappointment, the trend towards the certainties of Islam (and indeed a strong, but up to now generally ignored, revival of the monastic tradition among the Copts and a rise of militancy in originally anodyne movements such as Sunday schools) offers a refuge in simple, eternal truths from the complexities of a frustrating society. It is understandable, in these conditions, that an alienated society should seek to recreate the City of God and revert to a lost Golden Age.

24

The return to an Islamic culture can be seen most clearly in the direction of student enrolment, and in the types of programme broadcast by radio and television. Thus, three-quarters of university students study humanities. Within the humanities, there is a clear movement of students towards enrolment in the 'Islamic faculties'. These faculties are theology, Dar al'Ulum, Islamic legislature, Arabic Islamic Studies, Islamic Message, and the Islamic Faculty for Girls. Total enrolment in these faculties rose from 23,379 students in 1976–7 (8.52% of the total) to 77,409 in 1984–5 (11.34% of the total). The faculty of Islamic legislature in the Azhar, for instance, tripled its intake from 4,704 students in 1976–7 to 14,361 in 1984–5.[18]

Broadcasting has also witnessed an increase in religious programmes during the period 1977–82. Thus, although radio stations between them broadcast some 25 hours and 54 minutes of religious programmes per day in 1977, this figure increased to 31 hours and 12 minutes in 1984–5. As a proportion of total broadcasting, however, the share of religious programmes decreased during this period from 19.6% to 18.75%. The main type of radio broadcast continued to be comedy. Television broadcasting has also witnessed an increased interest in religious programmes, although this is less easy to identify than religious programmes on radio. Thus, overtly religious programmes increased only slightly: from 1 hour and 36 minutes a day in 1977 to 2 hours and 6 minutes a day in 1984–5, or 8.26% of total television programmes at the beginning of the period, and 8.75% at the end. But religion is broadcast through 'drama' programmes, as well as through overtly religious programmes, and these represent the bulk of television transmission and often include stories from early Islam – a dramatized Golden Legend. Similarly, 'cultural programmes' often deal with Islamic culture.[19]

In addition to the more obvious manifestations of alienation, Egyptians have exhibited a striking degree of indifference to the formal operation of political institutions. This is nowhere more clear than in the elections of 1987 (see Chapter 4). The participation rate in these elections was in the region of 25% to 30% for the population as a whole. This rate, however, dropped to as low a level as 14% in some areas of Cairo. In an opinion poll taken early in 1987, only 17.4% of the poorest agricultural workers knew which political parties existed in Egypt. The proportion rose to 37% for small and middle landowners, 51% for industrial workers, 62% for the lower echelons of government employees, 73% among middle-

and upper-echelon employees and 77% for students – the largest proportion in the sample group of 700. The sample was biased in favour of urban areas, especially in the Delta. Results of the opinion poll, however, suggest a positive correlation between education and income level and interest in the country's political life. Alienation appears greatest among those groups which are poor, have low levels of education and have seen the social promises of the state broken.[20]

The other noticeable effect of this alienation from the political process, and one which may well prove to be the most durable in the long run, is a widespread cynicism and loss of respect for a regime which has not kept its promises. This explains the generalized phenomenon of tax-evasion, the spread of bribery throughout society, the amusement with which remonstrations of such traditional authority figures as the policeman (*shawish*) are greeted by the majority of the population and the increase in the fortune of 'squarers' (*mukhalasati*) who, for a price, can cut through the maze of red tape as if by magic.

Conclusion and prospects

Throughout this paper, I have attempted to describe the disappointment of most of society in the failure of the post-1952 regime to fulfil its promises. This regime had based its legitimacy on, and indoctrinated the majority of the population with, the ideals of national independence, as well as 'Sufficiency and Justice'. The disappointment of the hopes of a generation in the achievement of these ideals led to its alienation from government and the perception that the government had failed in its self-imposed mission. It has been my contention that many of the social problems faced by Egypt today largely stem from alienation from, and loss of respect for, the state. Predictions, even for the near future, are notoriously dangerous, and only the most general will be attempted here. These are based upon two factors: first, the return of migrant labour from abroad in large numbers; and, second, a rise in the influence of religion as a determinant of politics.

The possibility of a large-scale return of Egyptian migrant labour from the oil-rich Arab countries, and indeed of the downturn in levels of labour migration, are together perhaps the most important factor of any. In addition to the economic effects of a reduction in workers' remittances, there would be significant social effects. In a report presented to the President of the Republic, the Higher Specialized Councils, an advisory body, consider two scenarios, one optimistic and one pessimistic. The optimistic one is based upon a 5% decrease in the number of Egyptians working in oil-rich states, and a 2.5% decrease in Egyptians working in the rest of the Arab world such as Jordan, Sudan and Yemen. The pessimistic scenario doubles the proportion of net returning migrants. Thus, in the report, the number of returning workers ranges from 40,000 a year to upwards of 80,000 in the worst-case scenario. These figures do not take into account Egyptians working in Iraq, or illegal emigration of labour.

Tentative figures for Libya alone, by the same agency, are in the region of some 29,000 returning labourers per annum. Of the total returning migrant labour, 27% will be employed in government and the public sector, where their return will have the effect of increasing disguised unemployment. The remainder will return to agriculture and the construction sector.[21] Some of the latter will presumably replace child labour, surely a desirable state of affairs, while others will displace women employed in these sectors – a much less desirable outcome but one which appears inevitable.

It appears, however, that in the event of generalized depression in neighbouring Arab countries, open unemployment is bound to rise, thereby increasing the size of an urban lumpenproletariat that is no longer capable of living in a rural environment, but has not yet adapted to urban conditions. This group is bound to form the bulk of any civil unrest, thus lending the Islamic opposition, recently on the rise, a critical mass which it has hitherto lacked. In the case of a worsening of the economic crisis (see Chapter 3), this urban lumpenproletariat of unemployed or semi-employed individuals, living on the fringes of legality from petty trade and personal services, may coalesce into a mob. Such a danger should not be discounted, since it may lead to a situation as dramatic as the burning of Cairo some 35 years ago.

The rise of political Islam and the increasing alienation and militancy of the Coptic minority are perhaps more immediate. It is clear that an Islamic ideology currently dominates the political arena, with even the government making concessions to the call for *shari'a* (Islamic law) as the organizing principle of society. But the opposition of Islamic protest movements to the government should not be overestimated. Representatives of these movements, led by the Muslim Brothers but not exclusively dominated by them, obtained 36 of the 458 seats in the 1987 general election. Apart from their slogan 'Islam is the solution', however, the rare concrete policies proposed by them have not differed substantially from those proposed by the government. Indeed, policies advocated by the Islamic opposition amount to little more than a crackdown on profiteering, and a cosmetic change in banking laws from 'interest rates' to their Islamic equivalent. The ideological power of these Islamic groups appears to be great, as does their capacity to channel the anger and frustration of the majority of the population. Despite this power, however, the situation looks to remain stable unless two conditions of the implicit social contract are breached.

First, the government should not be perceived by the majority of the population as compromising the country's honour. Shame and humiliation are explosive in a situation in which most people are sensitive to the issues of national pride and independence. In this respect, there is very little that the government can do. For instance, in the relationship with the United States, the major aid donor, the government must tread a wary path between compliance with American foreign policy, as well as the international aid donors' calls for domestic economic reform, and the risk of appearing to compromise on national independence and honour.

Perhaps this dilemma was seen at its clearest in the aftermath of the affair of the cruise ship *Achille Lauro* in October 1985. The Egyptair plane carrying the perpetrators of the hijack was in its turn intercepted and forced to land by US aircraft. Whether or not this was a justifiable course of action is beyond the scope of this essay. The fact remains that it was seen as an insult to Egyptian national sentiment, and provoked some localized demonstrations of outrage. Beyond expressing its 'hurt', however, there was not much that Egypt's government could do without alienating the major aid donor. On that occasion, the incident was ably managed by Egypt's president. Should similar events to the *Achille Lauro* occur in the future, Egypt's leaders will have their political skills, in both foreign and domestic policy, tested to the utmost.

Second, despite the fact that economic conditions are difficult, and becoming more so, an attitude of individualism and independence from the 'providential State' (in the religious sense of the term 'providence') appears to be gaining ground in Egyptian society, for the first time in many years. Popular anger in the form of spontaneous rioting will be aroused only in cases where the government is seen as behaving in a blatantly 'unjust' manner, for example, by increasing the service time of military conscripts or imposing dramatically higher prices on goods which, even if they are not always regarded as necessities, still retain a symbolic value. Thus, although the reports that subsidized bread is fed to livestock may be true, a dramatic increase in the price of bread to its international value would have a symbolic power and could be seen as emanating from an unjust, despotic state, while a slow deterioration in living standards would not necessarily be viewed in the same way. Revolt, in these conditions, and in terms of the *moral* discourse prevailing, would be justified.

The social situation in Egypt does not give cause for optimism. But neither is it desperate. There are signs that popular expectations of a paternalistic state are weakening. What is lacking today is a sense of direction. Without policies which can return to Egyptians this sense of direction, and which can channel feelings of national, cultural and religious pride into popular development programmes, any attempt by the authorities to capture the imagination of Egyptians, and even to govern the country, will remain a difficult and unenviable task.

Notes

1 Central Agency for Public Mobilization and Statistics, *Press Release* (mimeographed), Cairo, 1985, p. 1.
2 Roberto Aliboni, *et al.*, *Egypt's Economic Potential* (London: Croom Helm, 1984), pp. 168–9.
3 Ibrahim al-Issawi, *Fi Islah Ma Afsaduhu'l Infitah* (Cairo: Kitab al-Ahali, September 1984), p. 173, quoting an unnamed report of the International Labour Organization.
4 Ibid., p. 176.
5 Central Agency for Public Mobilization and Statistics, *Statistical Yearbook* (Cairo: August 1983), p. 7, and Aliboni, *op.cit.*, p. 168.
6 Arab Republic of Egypt, Shura Council, Minutes of 28 December 1982, p. 30.
7 *Ibid.*, Minutes of 4 March 1984, p. 96.
8 Reported in *al-Ahali*, 4 March 1987, p. 10.
9 Quoted in Aliboni, *op cit.*, pp. 174–5.
10 *Al-Wafd*, 16 April 1987, p. 7.

11 *Ibid., loc cit.*
12 CAPMAS, 1983, pp. 192–200. For recent figures, see CAPMAS, *Statistical Yearbook*, 1985, pp. 200ff.
13 Issawi, *op cit.*, p. 96.
14 Arab Republic of Egypt, Presidency of the Republic, The Higher Specialized Councils, *Taqrir al-Majlis al-Qawmi Lil Khadamat Wal Tanmiya'l Ijtima'iya* (Cairo: 1986), pp. 267–9.
15 *Ibid.*, p. 52.
16 Aliboni, *op cit.*, p. 191.
17 Higher Specialized Councils, *op cit.*, pp. 166–7, and Aliboni, *op cit.*, p. 175.
18 CAPMAS, 1983, pp. 192–8, and CAPMAS, *Statistical Yearbook*, 1986.
19 *Ibid.*, pp. 229 and 232.
20 Quoted in *al-Ahali*, 8 April 1987, p. 7.
21 Higher Specialized Councils, *op cit.*, p. 171.

3

THE ECONOMY

Ali Abdallah and Michael Brown*

Overview

Egypt's economic problems are now acute. Real growth has faltered since 1985, unemployment is a growing concern and the annual rate of inflation may be in excess of 30%. Egypt's principal sources of foreign exchange – oil, remittances, Suez Canal receipts and tourism – have been depressed by the collapse in the oil price and the associated recession in the Gulf. In consequence, both the fiscal and the external accounts have moved into large, and unsustainable, imbalance (see Tables 3.1 and 3.2 at the end of this chapter). Total external debt probably exceeds $45bn (Table 3.3), equivalent to 900% of exports of goods and services, and payments arrears were sizeable and increasing at end-1986.

The causes of Egypt's economic difficulties are deep-rooted. They include bureaucratic inefficiency, poor planning and inappropriate past policies resulting in cost/price distortions which have discouraged productive sectors and exports. These distortions were first masked and then brought into sharp focus by developments in the oil market. Furthermore, necessary adjustment has been delayed for

---

*Ali Abdallah and Michael Brown are pseudonyms for various economists who have given us advice on this chapter.

political reasons, and attempts to correct structural weaknesses have been partial and unsuccessful and provoked strong popular opposition.

Following the spring 1987 agreement on an International Monetary Fund (IMF) stand-by arrangement, fresh World Bank loans and the rescheduling of official debts, the Egyptian economy has been given a brief respite. The stage has at last been set to start the long process of economic reform. Yet the proposed measures do not appear tough enough, given the extent of the problems. The outlook for the balance of payments, in particular, and the economy as a whole is bleak, and could well remain so at least for the rest of this century.

The recent past

Egypt is no stranger to economic difficulties, as the historical record, including the Old Testament, bears out. Throughout its long history, the country has had to cope with the constraints of climate and geography, in particular a scarcity of cultivable land. Over the past 40 years, these natural constraints have been compounded by very rapid population growth, costly wars against Israel and disruptive shifts in economic strategy.

Many of Egypt's problems were exacerbated by developments under Nasser in the 1950s and 1960s, years of rapid industrialization through central planning and state control. The government intervened directly in most sectors, including industry, finance, construction and transport, and indirectly in agriculture. Economic innovations, such as a system of complex price controls and subsidies to protect the living standards of the urban population, were introduced. These policies swelled an already inefficient bureaucracy and public sector and led to growing weaknesses in resource allocation. By the late 1960s, economic growth was hesitant, and strains were emerging in public finances and the balance of payments, strains that were magnified by the 1967 and 1973 wars with Israel.

In late 1973, President Sadat shifted to a more outward-looking, 'open door' development policy (*infitah*), designed to encourage domestic and foreign private investment in Egypt. New laws and incentives were introduced, notably Law No. 43 of 1974, to improve the investment climate and assure investors of the government's commitment to the private sector; and closer political and economic ties were developed with the West and with the United States in particular (following the 1978 Camp David agreements). This policy had some success, for example in raising the private sector's share of industrial output and in creating a more open and competitive financial system through the establishment of over 50 branches and joint ventures by foreign banks. The economy also benefited substantially at this time from rising oil production and foreign aid. Yet despite attempts to streamline the public sector in the mid-1970s, little was achieved. Similarly, when reform of the government's finances was tried, it was not a success. A 1977 IMF programme was abandoned after reductions in subsidies led to food riots – an experience which subsequently deterred President Mubarak from making similar cuts in government spending.

Mubarak, who became president in 1981, began by calling for a 'national debate' on the pressing economic problems. But, in reality, the causes of the economic problems, such as inefficient government interference, were clear. Despite the priority given by the president to improving the economy, few of the tough political decisions required have been taken. Among such difficult policies are reform of the exchange system, reductions in subsidies and raising of interest rates to more realistic levels.

As long as external factors remained favourable, the economy continued to grow rapidly on the strength of rising foreign-exchange earnings from oil, remittances from migrant workers in the Gulf, tourism and Suez Canal dues, as well as foreign aid. But in 1985–6 oil prices collapsed and the region as a whole moved into recession. The main sources of Egypt's foreign exchange were sharply reduced (see Table 3.2), leaving major internal and external imbalances and making debt service unfinanceable.

Fundamental problems
Any reform programme for Egypt will have to address a number of fundamental problems, outlined below:

Population
The population has more than doubled in the past 30 years to 50 million in 1986. It is currently growing at the rate of one million every 8 or 9 months (or about 3% a year) and could reach 70 million by the end of the century (see Table 3.4). As the death rate has halved

in the past 30 years, the rate of population growth has become more rapid. Since only 3%-4% of Egypt's land is currently habitable or cultivable, the country is now one of the most densely populated in the world.

This is a major constraint on policy-makers. The pressure of population, coupled with the urban drift of recent years, has put considerable strains on infrastructure and basic services in the main cities. Scarce cultivable land is used for housing when it is badly needed for food production. Urban unemployment, and underemployment, is a serious social as well as economic concern, particularly as the large number of new entrants to the labour force is being augmented by returning migrant workers from the Gulf. Yet any programmes or policies advocating birth control are highly controversial in a predominantly Islamic country; the authorities also have difficulty overcoming the natural view (in a poor country) that children are an insurance against old age. Moreover, children play a significant role in the agricultural sector, in which, as a result of urban drift, there are labour shortages, particularly at harvest time.

Despite the strains on the economy imposed by rapid population growth, the sheer size of Egypt's population can be viewed as an asset in the longer term. A large population provides industry with a viable domestic market, which is not the case in other Arab countries. It also provides a source of cheap labour, which could be put to productive use in agriculture, for example, or in factories financed by capital from the West or the Gulf States. Returning migrant workers are bringing back capital as well as some skills, and there is scope for new, small businesses in several sectors, as experience since Sadat's reforms shows. But, as will be discussed in a later section, it will not be easy to exploit this potential unless Egypt's more immediate problems are tackled.

Agriculture and food production

Although, as Table 3.5 shows, agriculture is still the largest sector in the economy in terms of employment (35%) and contribution to GDP (16%), it has declined in relative importance since the mid-1970s, when it accounted for 30% of GDP. Growth has fallen well behind other sectors and the economy as a whole; and agricultural production, currently rising by 2% per annum, has not kept pace with population growth, now around 3% per annum. From being self-sufficient in food and a net exporter of agricultural commodities in the early 1970s, Egypt now has an annual net deficit of $3bn on agricultural trade.

The sector has suffered from several factors. Despite government efforts to reclaim desert land, the area under cultivation has remained more or less constant for many years as reclamation has been offset by the diversion of agricultural land for other uses, especially housing. Further attempts at reclamation are unlikely to be economic owing to the high cost (perhaps several thousand dollars per acre), the poor quality of much of the land left unreclaimed (a fact recognized as long ago as 1966 in a Food and Agriculture Organization report) and the scarcity of water following years of low rainfall. Additionally, the reduced size of land holdings, following Nasser's agrarian reforms, makes Egypt generally unsuitable for some forms of mechanization, such as the use of tractors.

Most importantly, agriculture has been subject to extensive state intervention. The government has provided key inputs, determined cultivation patterns, fixed output prices and set distribution and marketing controls. These controls, aimed at providing cheap food for urban consumers, have failed to create adequate incentives for producers and distorted the pattern of agricultural output. Low and inflexible producer prices have led to a shift away from cotton, rice and sugar towards more remunerative crops such as animal fodder, which may be less efficient from the country's overall economic standpoint.

Exports have also been discouraged by a systematically overvalued exchange rate. Any incentive to adopt more appropriate pricing policies has been considerably lessened by the ready availability of heavily subsidized wheat imports from the West. Yet if farmers were offered more adequate incentives, and if the flow of population out of the countryside were halted, agricultural output could be greatly improved.

Industry

Many African Third World countries have been criticized for trying to diversify out of agriculture. But, given the natural constraints on Egypt's agricultural capacity, it is difficult to criticize Egypt for trying to industrialize. With an urbanized population that is relatively well educated by comparison with other countries in Africa, and with the wealthy Gulf States willing to invest in Arab countries, Egypt's industrial capabilities appear comparatively good. Indeed these advantages seemed to have been harnessed during the 1970s and early 1980s, when industrial production rose at an annual rate of around 10%.

However, industrial growth slowed markedly in 1985–6, owing mainly to growing foreign-exchange constraints. Moreover, the earlier expansion concealed important weaknesses. It was based, in large part, on heavy protection and government subsidies, including loans at negative real interest rates (and sometimes in artificially cheap foreign exchange) to industry (including public enterprises, which continue to dominate the sector). Despite the surge in private manufacturing since 1973–4, public-sector enterprises still accounted for two-thirds of the value of industrial output in 1984/5* (compared with three-quarters in the mid-1970s). Their financial performance has been and remains weak, reflecting high costs, loss of skilled labour to neighbouring Gulf countries, rapidly increasing costs of foreign currency debt service and rigid price controls. Many public-sector businesses appear inefficient and unprofitable. Some newly established private companies, which came 'on stream' after the economy went into recession, are also in financial difficulties.

More generally, the industrial base has remained relatively narrow, and the objective of import substitution has been only partially achieved. Exports have been held back by overvalued exchange rates and by trade and fiscal policies which have favoured production for the domestic market. Government efforts notwithstanding, including the recent establishment of an Export Development Bank, industrial exports (mainly textiles, metallurgical and engineering goods) were equivalent to only 7% of the value of industrial production in 1984/5.

Public sector
The public sector, which consists of the central and local governments, public authorities and public companies, is large in size, complex in structure and inefficient in practice. There are no less than 46 economic authorities and 372 public-sector companies, supervised by 18 different ministries. As in the industrial sector (see above), many of these bodies are overstaffed, poorly managed and loss-making. They have become employers of last resort for university graduates and ex-military personnel; and low wages, relative to the private sector, have meant a high turnover of qualified staff.

*Most published Egyptian data relate to fiscal years ending 30 June.

Pervasive government controls on the prices of public-sector products have been a major constraint on profitability. Substantial subsidies, implicit and explicit, have made public enterprises a major drain on scarce budgetary resources. Accountability has also been weak, allowing enterprises to run up sizeable arrears and/or borrow in foreign currency without adequate regard to debt-servicing capacity.

This overcentralized, top-heavy structure, a legacy of Nasser, is superimposed on a centuries-old bureaucratic tradition, combining delay and corruption in equal measure. The present bureaucracy is no different, being resistant to change, low-paid and often of low calibre. Procedures are cumbersome and decision-making a lengthy and often frustrating process. The customs administration, in particular, is notorious for its inefficiency and corruption. Lack of coordinated policy-making and of exchanges of information between individual ministries has impeded planning and has led to erratic implementation of controls and subsidies.

One of the main problems of the bureaucracy is that ability is not rewarded and promotions are granted on the basis of seniority. Although assessments are made of civil servants' performance, these are virtually meaningless because supervisors tend to give the highest rating ('excellent') irrespective of the person's competence. Thus in 1986, the Central Agency for Organization and Administration, which administers the whole bureaucracy, rated 92% of its staff in the 'excellent' category.

Foreign aid and external borrowing
Over the past decade, the economy has become heavily dependent on aid and external borrowing, a dependence which has delayed domestic reforms and encouraged the belief that others will always come to Egypt's rescue. In the 1970s, aid from Arab oil-producing states increased significantly, averaging over $1bn a year between 1973 and 1979. After the signing of the peace treaty with Israel in 1979, the United States became the main donor and now provides some $2bn annually, with a further $1bn coming from the World Bank and other Western countries, notably France and Germany, in various forms. Egypt has also borrowed heavily to finance current spending, and outstanding external debts are estimated at over $45bn (including military loans). Because of balance-of-payments deficits and very low foreign-exchange reserves (equivalent to less

than one month's imports at end-January 1987), this debt can no longer be serviced. By late 1986, arrears had risen to $6bn.

Immediate problems

External

These structural weaknesses were hidden in the decade after 1975 by the marked rise in foreign-exchange earnings, particularly from higher oil production and high oil prices, which had a major impact on the economy. In 1973 oil constituted less than 4% of GDP, but by 1984/5 it accounted for 20%, as well as two-thirds of merchandise exports and a quarter of current-account receipts.

In 1985/6, however, the dramatic fall in oil prices reduced Egypt's oil receipts sharply. This was exacerbated by the Egyptian General Petroleum Corporation's poor marketing and uncompetitive pricing. Oil exports were very low in the first part of 1986, and oil receipts fell by around $1bn in 1985/6 to $2bn. Although the oil market firmed in the first half of 1987, the outlook for prices remains uncertain; and while exploration is going ahead in partnership with foreign companies, present reserves are only 4.8bn barrels, sufficent to last only ten years at current rates of production.

The decline in oil receipts was accompanied by a sharp fall in workers' remittances, a consequence of recession and a shakeout of expatriate labour in the Gulf. Although accurate figures are unobtainable, because of substantial unrecorded flows through the free market, officially recorded remittances may have fallen from about $3.5bn in 1984/5 to $3bn in 1985/6. They could fall further as the Gulf economies face a period of consolidation. The current Saudi Arabian Five-Year Plan, for example, aims at reducing foreign workers by 600,000 over the period to 1990. Iraq, which remains financially hard-pressed by the Gulf war, has already reduced its Egyptian workforce from one million to 600,000 and could make further cuts. Moreover, since the early 1980s, salaries in the Gulf have fallen sharply – by around 30% – for those expatriates who remain abroad.

Tourism was also affected adversely in 1985/6 by the Gulf recession, which reduced the number of Arab visitors, and by concerns about security in the region. Western tourists, in particular, were deterred by the *Achille Lauro* incident in October 1985 and the

February 1986 Security Police riots in Cairo. Official receipts from tourism (perhaps only a third of total tourist receipts) are estimated to have fallen by 25% to $0.3bn in 1985–6. Nonetheless, a recovery was under way by early 1987, and tourist facilities are now being actively developed with greater private-sector participation. The mid-1987 depreciation in the official exchange rate (see below) should also encourage more tourist receipts to go through the banking system. The government hopes that tourism will generate earnings of $2.5bn a year within five years. The industry is certainly one in which Egypt appears to enjoy a comparative advantage.

Although Suez Canal dues remained stable in dollar terms, at around $1bn a year, the decline in the other major sources of foreign exchange led to a widening in the current-account deficit (excluding aid) to around $4bn in 1985/6 (see Table 3.2). This brought into sharp focus the inherent distortions and inefficiencies of the multiple-exchange-rate regime, which had become increasingly complex to administer. For several years, overvalued and unrepresentative official rates for specified transactions, supported by bureaucratic restrictions, encouraged a high volume of imports, which the country could not afford, at the expense of export production. They also produced an active parallel market with further loss of potential foreign-exchange earnings.

Reforms have been tried in the past, but they have only tinkered with the system, often increasing its complexity and resulting in failure. In January 1985, for example, the government tried to eliminate the free market by prohibiting the private sector from importing through this market. Unauthorized foreign-currency dealers were arrested, and private firms were forced to pay for imports at a newly introduced commercial bank exchange rate. But this rate was set too low to attract foreign exchange into the commercial banks, which were thus unable to meet the foreign-exchange needs of private importers. In April 1985, only three months after its implementation, the reform was rescinded. If the exchange system is to be reformed successfully, a unified, flexible and market-related exchange system will have to be introduced, as envisaged in the 1987 IMF programme.

Domestic
Public finances have also deteriorated in the early 1980s, with budget deficits equivalent to around 20% of GDP. Revenue performance

has been weak, owing in part to poor tax collection procedures and the low elasticity of the tax system relative to domestic income, and current outlays have increased substantially (including interest payments on domestic borrowing, which tripled between 1981/2 and 1985/6). Subsidies are a major problem. As well as their direct cost, £E2.8bn per year between 1983/4 and 1985/6, their indiscriminate application has wasted scarce resources. Some 97% of the population have ration cards, despite conspicuous affluence in some sections. Egypt has the highest per capita loaf consumption in the world; and subsidized bread is reportedly used as animal fodder. Despite periodic reform plans, bureaucratic inefficiency and political pressures have meant that subsidies have not been targeted effectively at the needy.

Similar distortions stem from the subsidies on domestic oil products and electricity prices, which are priced far below world market levels. This has led to continued high domestic oil consumption, about 40% of total output, reducing potential export earnings, while at the same time encouraging 'luxury' imports of consumer goods such as private cars. The great numbers of these last are now clogging up the main cities, necessitating heavy expenditure on infrastructure and again diverting oil products from export markets.

High government spending has been financed, in large part, by increasing borrowing from domestic banks. This has contributed to rapid growth in the monetary aggregates and high inflation. Interest rates on Egyptian pound deposits have remained negative in real terms, and are now sharply so, which has made borrowing 'cheap' and reduced the incentive for domestic savings. Negative interest rates, coupled with unrealistic exchange rates and a general weakness of confidence, have also led to a rapid increase in the use of foreign currency for domestic transactions.

Egyptian banks now have sizeable domestic liabilities in convertible currencies equivalent to about 40% of total deposits. This sharply reduces the scope for an active monetary policy. Even the banks' net convertible currency liabilities, at more than $3bn, far exceed the level of the Central Bank's foreign-exchange holdings. This leaves the banks vulnerable to a devaluation, which could undermine their capital structure, and to loss of confidence by depositors, particularly since the Central Bank, with its small holdings of foreign currency, could not provide much support as lender of last resort.

On top of this, the Central Bank has to decide how to deal with the growing phenomenon of Islamic financial institutions, which pay 'dividends' rather than 'interest' on deposit and do not guarantee the value of deposits. There are currently three Islamic banks (compared with around 60 'Western-style' banks), and the largest, Faisal Islamic Bank, has built up over $2bn of assets in nine years. The Nasser Social Bank, founded fifteen years ago, is Egypt's oldest Islamic bank; and the Islamic International Bank for Investment and Development, founded in 1981, has already emerged as a significant force.

Yet it is the influence of the Islamic investment companies that is causing most concern. They have attracted large deposits (perhaps 15%-20% of all Egyptian deposits) by offering high dividends, often financed by speculation in gold, foreign currency and commodities. Al-Rayan, Egypt's largest investment company, has been offering annual rates of return of 20%-30% (compared with 8.5% on commercial bank three-month deposit rates), and claims to have attracted deposits from over 300,000 individual depositors. But Islamic institutions have frequently been accused of making risky and injudicious business decisions: at the end of 1986 there was a run on al-Rayan when press rumours claimed the company had lost $100mn through speculating in gold.

In recent months, the Central Bank has moved to try and control the spread of Islamic investment activities. In June 1987, for example, the Central Bank blocked al-Rayan's attempt to buy Bank of America's 40% share in Misr America International Bank; and it has also stalled the Saudi-based al-Baraka group's plans to buy a 46% stake in the local Pyramids Bank and convert it to Islamic principles. By taking a firm stand, the authorities risk provoking powerful fundamentalist Muslim opposition. Yet failure to do so could jeopardize the stability of the financial system on which a successful diversified economy will depend.

Reform

Given the nature and extent of the problems, President Mubarak has turned to the IMF, the World Bank and official creditors for a multilateral solution. He has, however, done so reluctantly because of unease about the social and political implications of adjustment. Mubarak is concerned, particularly in view of the 1977 food riots, that the fundamentalists, who gained seats in the April 1987 parliamentary elections, could exploit the fall in GDP per capita of probably some 6% between 1986 and 1988. Discussions about reform have therefore been drawn out and Mubarak has consistently sought to soften the proposals. It is widely thought he dismissed Prime Minister Lutfi and Central Bank Governor Negm in late 1986 because they accepted the IMF's prescribed austerity too readily. Mubarak has also explored alternative solutions, such as a short-lived proposal for a Middle East Regional Economic Plan in mid-1986, and has tried to cover immediate requirements with new Arab aid.

Despite these doubts and delays, major creditors are anxious to maintain stability in such a strategically important country and have taken a generally sympathetic attitude to Egypt's problems in the IMF. Egypt signed a formal Letter of Intent with the IMF in February 1987, and an 18-month stand-by arrangement for approximately $325mn was approved in May 1987. This was accompanied by rescheduling on generous terms of official debts (including military) supported by new loans from the World Bank and other donors to close the remaining financing gap.

In May 1987, Western creditors at the Paris Club agreed to reschedule substantial debts, variously estimated at between $7bn and $12bn, over 10 years with five years' grace. Agreement with the USSR had already been reached, in March 1987, to reschedule $2–3bn of military debts on even more favourable terms, with all interest waived. Creditors have also said that they will react generously to requests for new funds, and stand ready to discuss further reschedulings in support of IMF programmes.

In return for this financing package, Egypt is having to implement important policy changes. The authorities have promised to unify, in a three-stage process, the multiple exchange system. Under the first phase, introduced in May 1987, 40% of transactions, including workers' remittances and tourist expenditures, have been transferred from the commercial bank pool to a new market-related rate that is set daily by a committee of bank representatives (the rate was set initially at £E2.17 = $1). The aim is to transfer a further 40% of transactions to the new rate by end-December 1987, and the remainder by end-June 1988.

The authorities are also committed to reducing the fiscal deficit from the 16% of GDP projected in the 1986/7 budget to 13% of

GDP in 1987/8 (see Table 3.1), with the aim of eventually phasing it out altogether, although no time-table has been set for this. In addition, monetary policy is to be tightened somewhat, with restrictions on domestic bank credit and interest rates rising by two percentage points. (The IMF backed down from its original demand that interest rates be doubled or trebled to match inflation of around 30%.)

Egypt's new Five-Year Plan (1987/8–1991/2) is designed to tackle the economy's structural problems with support from the World Bank. The aim is to give the private sector a greater role in productive activities, and to improve the efficiency and quality of the state sector by means of a £E26.5bn public-sector investment programme, channelled particularly into energy and manufacturing. The Plan forecasts these improvements will lead to an annual growth rate of 5.8% – but this looks highly optimistic given the poor short-term economic prospects of the region as a whole. It will also be difficult to find the external and domestic funds necessary to finance the ambitious investment programme, even though the World Bank may increase its rate of loan disbursements significantly. Moreover, bureaucratic ability and motivation will be required (qualities that are currently lacking) if the Plan is to be put into practice.

Outlook

With the IMF programme and the rest of the package in place, Egypt should gain a much-needed respite, at least in the short term. Thereafter much depends on the strength of Egypt's own adjustment efforts, some of which have now begun. Tariffs were liberalized in 1986 and agricultural producer prices have been increased. In May 1987 the first stage of exchange reform was introduced, and domestic energy prices were raised, although they remain considerably below world market levels. Exchange reform has got off to a reasonable start, mainly because the new, free-market bank rate was set, and has been maintained, at a competitive level. Yet the arrest of many unauthorized foreign-exchange dealers suggests that the authorities may not have learned the lesson of 1985, namely that a parallel market can act as a safety valve. The arrests have also inhibited the operations of the foreign banks, in particular, by depriving them and their customers of a principal source of foreign exchange.

Clearly, however, the authorities are attempting to tackle important problems. An optimist could argue that the country's potential, particularly in agriculture and tourism, remains largely unutilized. With appropriate policies to encourage the private sector and attract finance from abroad, Egypt could go some way towards reviving its economy and restoring its international creditworthiness. When the IMF reviews the stand-by towards the end of 1987, stricter targets may be introduced. If the current programme were to be adhered to, and future programmes were to follow on, it is possible that reform could show positive results.

Yet many observers are sceptical on several counts. First, the economy is vulnerable to exogenous shocks – the oil price being a prime example – which could undermine the whole programme. Second, these observers doubt whether the Egyptian government's heart is really in the reform programme. They fear Mubarak will retract the austerity measures, as Sadat did in 1977, when domestic hardship begins to bite. Third, even if the government sticks to the IMF programme, it is doubtful that the economy can recover sufficiently to meet debt-service obligations when grace periods on the rescheduled debt expire. The IMF medicine is of the right type, but the dosage may not be strong enough to give creditors the confidence to promote new investment.

Even if the IMF programme is adhered to, the current-account deficit (excluding aid) could *rise* by 50% by 1991/2 to over $6bn. If all goes well, therefore, it will take at least a decade to rectify existing imbalances. Moreover, the level of debt that will by then have accumulated means that restoring the economy to self-sustaining growth may be postponed until the next century, a prospect with daunting implications both for the Egyptians and for their friends and supporters abroad. At best, the West faces the prospect of years of rescheduling and continuing large aid donations.

But all may not go well. The problems are so deep-rooted that the changes needed to redress them may be too difficult, politically and administratively, to carry through. The current IMF programme could easily fail. This would leave unsolved the problems of a massive debt burden, an inefficient industry, a stifling bureaucracy and rapid population growth. Egypt would then have to try to continue 'muddling through', becoming even more dependent on

US and Gulf aid, a course that would erode Egypt's long-standing desire to regain a dominant and independent role in regional politics. In this scenario, as living standards (and national self-esteem) declined, the probability would be that capital and skills would continue to emigrate, further weakening the economy. Such a situation could provide fertile ground for political and religious extremists.

This scenario is not at all encouraging for Egypt's Western allies. If reform is aborted, they would face the choice of continuing to provide large-scale financial support (see Table 3.6) with no assurance that it would be effectively utilized, or of stopping aid with the risk of economic decay and domestic political unrest. One consequence might be the re-emergence of Soviet influence, although even the USSR might be reluctant to accept such a financial incubus, particularly given its earlier loss of influence and its inability to obtain repayment of previous military loans. If these risks are to be avoided, Egypt will have to undertake fundamental action now.

Some academics, at least, have considered radical solutions and have argued that creditors can be repaid and living standards maintained, but only at the cost of sharply cutting back investment expenditure so that GDP growth is broadly in line with population growth over the next decade. Such a policy would imply that Egypt was giving up Nasser's goal of becoming an industrialized nation. The fact that such views are being voiced, and occasionally listened to, indicates the extent of the predicament now facing Egypt's economy.

Statistical annex

The following tables have been compiled from various official sources and from estimates by the authors. By way of general introduction, it should be noted that the total land area of Egypt is 997,739 square kilometres, of which 35,200 square kilometres are inhabited and cultivated. Per capita GNP is $700, and the estimated population at the end of 1985 was 48.6 million.

Table 3.1 Budgetary developments (in £Ebn)

	1987/8	1986/7	1985/6
Total revenue	14.0	12.4	12.0
of which: (Tax)	(9.5)	(7.3)	(6.5)
Total expenditure	21.1	19.6	19.8
of which: (Wages)	(4.1)	(3.8)	(3.4)
(Subsidies)	(2.5)	(2.2)	(2.8)
(Investment spending)	(5.6)	(6.3)	(6.4)
Overall deficit	7.1	7.2	7.9
(as percentage of GDP)	(13%)	(16%)	(22%)

Table 3.2 Balance of payments (in $mn)

	1985/6 (estimate)	1983/4	1981/2
Sources of foreign exchange			
Visible exports	3,300	4,000	4,100
of which: (Petroleum)	(2,000)	(2,600)	(3,000)
Invisible exports	6,600	7,900	5,700
of which: (Workers' remittances)	(2,700)	(3,900)	(2,100)
(Suez Canal)	(1,000)	(1,000)	(900)
(Tourism)	(300)	(300)	(400)
Official transfers	1,200	800	100
TOTAL	11,100	12,700	9,900
Uses of foreign exchange			
Visible imports	9,600	10,700	9,000
Invisible imports	4,400	4,100	3,500
TOTAL	14,000	14,800	12,500
Trade deficit	6,300	6,700	4,900
Current-account deficit (incl. official transfers)	2,900	2,100	2,600
Current-account deficit (excl. official transfers)	4,100	2,900	2,700

Table 3.3 Growth in external debt (in $bn)

	1987	1986	1985	1984	1983
Outstanding debt	45.5	43.5	39.5	36.5	29.0

Table 3.4 Population growth

Year	Total population* (in millions)	Birth rate per thousand people	Death rate per thousand people	Rate of population growth (%)
1955	22.99	40.3	17.6	2.27
1965	29.40	41.5	14.0	2.75
1975	36.95	36.1	12.1	2.40
1985	48.59	37.4	9.1	2.97

*Figures include 2–3 million Egyptian nationals abroad.

Table 3.5 Components of GDP (as percentage of total)

	1985/6	1981/2
Commodity-producing sectors	51.8	51.7
of which: (Agriculture)	(16.3)	(19.1)
(Industry and mining)	(14.9)	(13.6)
(Petroleum)	(15.1)	(13.6)
Production services	28.5	28.6
of which: (Trade)	(12.2)	(12.4)
(Finance and insurance)	(7.1)	(7.1)
(Suez Canal)	(2.3)	(3.3)
Services	19.7	19.7
(Housing, tourism, etc.)		
TOTAL	100.0	100.0

Table 3.6 Breakdown of public-sector foreign debt (in $bn)

	end June 1986	end June 1984
USA	7.60	6.50
Other Western countries	10.00	5.50
Comecon and China	0.95	0.60
Arab and Islamic countries	3.55	3.40
Arab aid agencies	2.70	2.60
IMF, World Bank	2.80	2.15
Local and regional banks	1.55	1.50
Unallocated items	1.15	0.95
TOTAL	30.30*	23.20*

*On top of these figures, there would be around $2.7bn of private-sector debt and $10.0bn of military debt (mostly owed to the USA and USSR).

4

DOMESTIC POLITICS

Nazih N. Ayubi*

It is remarkable how stable the Egyptian political system has
remained over many years, in spite of its numerous and escalating
problems. The reasons for this are multiple: a political culture that is
both bureaucratic and constitutional in its own way, a political-
security machine that has grown very much in size and sophistica-
tion, and – especially since Mubarak – a populace that is no more
certain than its leader about where it wants to go. Having lived
through a semblance of both socialism (under Nasser) and capitalism (under Sadat), neither of which has delivered, nobody seems to
be sure where to go next. The same applies to foreign policy issues:
the country has lived with the Arabs, and lived, more or less, without
them; it felt the heavy hand of the Soviets and experienced the arm-
twisting of the Americans. None of the options has been without
pain. Only the religious militants seem to know what they want:
'Islam *is* the solution', they cry, but their intellectual concerns
remain as vague operationally and as marginal to the details of

*Nazih N. Ayubi is in the Department of Politics, University of Exeter.

modern life as ever. Stability is therefore to some extent the function of inertia, and of a perceived lack of alternatives.

The social base of the state

More profoundly, the static – but confused – situation can be attributed to the uncertain nature of the social base of the state, which reflects the combined outcomes of both Nasserist and Sadatist policies. While the state bourgeoisie of Nasser's socialist era is still in control of the government machine and a large part of the national economy, the commercial bourgeoisie of Sadat's *infitah* (open door) era is in control of a thriving parallel economy of finance and trade. The relationship between the two elements is complex, for although the regime's declared policy is economic liberalization, this very often runs counter to the interests of important segments of the bureaucratic establishment. And although several symbiotic relationships have developed between elements of the state bourgeoisie and elements of the commercial bourgeoisie, the two are by no means in full or continuous alliance. As the political leadership tries to play the role of arbiter between the sometimes conflicting interests and policies of the two fractions of the middle class, elements of vagueness, hesitation and contradiction often develop within the declared policies of the regime, resulting in slow, indecisive action or in reversal of policies.

The present state system has its origins in the Nasserist period, when the bureaucracy was consolidated and the economy was first 'Egyptianized', and then – for the most part – 'nationalized'. Although the Nasserist state may have reflected, to an extent, the aspirations of a rising middle class whose expectations had perhaps been blocked, that state in many ways created its *own* class base. A corporatist formula expanded and benefited an increasingly controlled labour force, while at the same time promoting to social eminence a military-technocratic elite.[1]

An inherent weakness in this system was the ultimate contradiction that was bound to develop between the regime's étatist and populist orientations and the opposing functions it was trying to combine: development versus welfare; production versus distribution. These difficulties began to emerge in the mid-1960s and were accentuated by the military defeat in the Six-Day War of 1967. A split within the state bourgeoisie developed, leading by the mid-

1970s – and under the impact of the oil boom – to the pre-eminence of the so-called 'Sadatist' branch that preferred an indirectly interventionist role for the state.[2] The adoption of *infitah* at this time was not in any large measure the work of a hibernating entrepreneurial class waiting for investment opportunity, nor was it simply an inevitable adjustment to the new requirements of the international division of labour; rather, it was a 'master policy' initiated by the Egyptian state itself to preserve its étatist economic role at a time of changing domestic and external circumstances.[3]

In terms of political movement, the state and its ruling elites have managed to introduce a number of socio-economic transformations through complex processes of conflict and alliance. These can be summarized as follows:[4]

– In the early 1970s, the Sadatist regime managed (especially with the 'Corrective Revolution' of May 1971) to rid itself of leaders of the Nasserist trend who defended the 'socialist gains' and the general framework of national state capitalism. The war of October 1973 enabled the new leadership to silence the main sources of popular and nationalist discontent.

– By the mid-1970s, the new leadership had managed to achieve relative independence from the political and social forces that were associated with the Nasserist era; this allowed it, on the one hand, to promulgate the *infitah* laws (reviving all latent elements of capitalism) and, on the other, to introduce some daring changes in Egypt's international alliances by dismantling its ties with the socialist countries and consolidating links with the United States and the West.

– In the second half of the 1970s, the leadership started to relax political restrictions and to allow a certain degree of diversification in political organizations. The aim was dual: to encourage foreign capital to invest in Egypt, and to rearrange ties and alliances so as to form the broadest possible front for the encirclement of Nasserist and socialist trends. Thus 'platforms' and parties emerged in 1976–7, and the Islamic trend was encouraged. However, social forces associated with the Nasserist period, along with others, expressed their anger so forcefully in the food riots that occurred all over Egypt in January 1977 that the regime had to retract many of its liberal promises and to apply considerable caution in its moves to develop a multi-party system.

– In the period following 1977, the limited ability of *infitah* to stimulate a real capitalist growth that would be led by the national bourgeoisie began to be clear, and the state resorted to new methods of maintaining its grip on society and of directing its economic transformation (although in a way that would not completely discourage foreign capital). In this period it became evident that the leadership lacked sympathy for national capitalism, as the state stepped back from its previously expressed intention of 'selling' the public sector to local investors. A virtually total divorce from Arab capital (and even from the Arab states themselves) was achieved following Sadat's visit to Jerusalem and the peace treaty (1977–9). The leadership headed instead for a direct partnership between the industrial public sector and foreign capital.

– By the early 1980s, it was apparent that peace with Israel had led neither to a softening of Israel's attitude nor to prosperity for the Egyptian economy. In addition, the Islamic movement began to realize that it had been used in a game that did not serve its own direct interests. Manifestations of popular discontent (especially in the form of workers' strikes) were increasing, as were sectarian skirmishes, and the Islamic movement began to escalate the acts of violence that reached their climax in 1981 with the assassination of Sadat.

By the end of the 1970s, Sadat had become the established leader of the Egyptian state bourgeoisie in fulfilling its new role. Unable to combine a development/welfare function but at the same time unwilling to give up its privileges in power and wealth, this state bourgeoisie was endeavouring to do the following:

(a) disentangle the ideological and political link between its developmental and its welfare roles, and encourage the public sector to seek profits and to give up its welfare activities;

(b) increase rentier types of income for the state, in specific instances, and for society at large (what accrued to the state could then be used to provide the minimum of welfare, e.g. basic consumer subsidies, without which political security would be at risk; and what accrued to individuals would, it was hoped, encourage them to look for other providers than the state); and

(c) make overtures to foreign investors, and seek partnerships between the public sector and international capitalism in joint ventures.

This last pushed the local middle class even further in the direction of commercial/financial activities as one of the very few outlets remaining open to it (especially since private merchants had easier access to the remittances of the millions of Egyptians working abroad). Indeed, the commercial/financial middle class became ruthless in defending its privileges, as became clear, for example, in early 1985 when its representatives managed to defeat new laws that were meant to mobilize the available monetary resources, through the formal banking system, for the benefit of the state.

The social base for this change in direction was a realignment of classes that brought to the fore an alliance among elements from the pre-revolutionary semi-aristocracy, the state bourgeoisie of the 1960s and the commercial/financial cliques of the *infitah* era.[5] Yet it should be clear that the role of the state bourgeoisie has not really been seriously reduced, since the state machinery remains large and continues to allocate to itself a significant proportion of national resources.[6] In particular, a considerable expansion in the state's organs of control and repression has been taking place since the 1970s (e.g. the Central Security Forces, the State Security Courts and the 'Morals' Courts, the Public Prosecutor's functions, as well as the bureaucracy, the armed forces, and the state information machine in general). Furthermore, much of the growth in bureaucratic expenditure in recent years has been directed to the country's higher political and administrative echelons.[7]

It should also be clear that the commercial middle class has started to acquire a life of its own. Although the state machine is amenable to the interests of the newly emerged class conglomeration of *infitah*, it does strive to play the role of arbiter among the various fractions of the evolving bourgeoisie, and even to maintain a certain degree of 'relative autonomy' vis-à-vis the conflicting class interests in society. Because of this, the state appears from time to time to reach a point of confrontation with the commercial/financial bourgeoisie, particularly when attempts are made, for example, to rationalize importation practices, free-zone activities or pricing policies.

One can say, in summary, that political power in Egypt is still basically in the hands of the state bourgeoisie, and that, although the state machine supports the general movement of private capital in society and even embarks on partnerships with it in several activities, it is still trying to keep aloof from the immediate narrow interests of the various capitalist fractions – a stance that has brought it into direct confrontation with the commercial bourgeoisie on a number of occasions. Nevertheless, since the general movement of private capital under the policy of *infitah* seems primarily to hurt several popular sectors outside the state machine, or on its fringes, the resistance that such sectors express against the emerging capitalism tends to take the form of rebellion against the state and confrontation with its institutions.

The Mubarak leadership style

President Mubarak has inherited a complex legacy from the Nasser and Sadat eras. Such a legacy is a mixed blessing: on the one hand it puts at his disposal an array of laws, institutions and practices that tend to work in favour of the head of state; on the other, it burdens him with the responsibility for outcomes of state policies that were initiated before his term (e.g. the emergence of the so-called '*infitah* mafia'). Thus, if he does not change these policies and institutions, they count as his own.

An Egyptian president enjoys tremendous powers, especially under the existing emergency laws. Egypt is a presidential state, and the Arabic term for the presidency (*riyasah*) connotes both powerful headship and affectionate bonds. All executive authority is vested constitutionally in the presidency: the President appoints the Cabinet (there is no mention of parliamentary majorities), is the Supreme Commander of the armed forces, and is the chief policy-maker in matters of security, diplomacy and the economy. The President is also by convention the head of the only permitted and/or the actually dominant political party.

Sadat added to all this a strong paternalistic touch by regarding himself as the 'Elder of the Egyptian Family', and by addressing all institutions in the possessive as 'my parliament', 'my army', 'my press'. He resorted too frequently to popular referenda to endorse his actions, amended the constitution in 1980 to make the number of presidential terms unlimited, and added to the legislature a second chamber (the Consultative Council), which is closely controlled by the ruling party.[8] In the view of one close observer, by the end of Sadat's presidency 'Egypt had reverted to an institutionalized one-party system'.[9]

President Mubarak has chosen not to use these extensive presidential powers either to alter the composition of the ruling elite or to make important shifts in the socio-economic system along the lines of Nasser's socialist changes or Sadat's *infitah*. He continues to muddle along, pursuing basically the same policies as his predecessor (*infitah* and 'peace') and relying on the same political party.

There were a few flirtations with certain aspects of Nasserism, and there was a short-lived campaign against corruption, but the regime has continued with basically the same personnel from the Sadat era. A minor degree of discipline was imposed on the policy of *infitah*, although its main thrust remains unchanged, a degree of rapprochement began to be achieved with other Arab countries but without sacrificing the 1979 Egyptian-Israeli peace treaty, and a measure of political liberalization was introduced, with some (but not all) political parties being allowed to function, but with the tight grip of the government and security apparatus making it clear who would continue to rule.

All in all, the Mubarak leadership has adopted a low-key, businesslike style, and, in addition to its reputation for honesty and clean-handedness, it has been quite careful and discreet in its approach to issues and problems. Mubarak's style seems unlikely to generate strong emotions among the populace, but it appears well suited to a society that has reached something of a crossroads in its development.

Mubarak has made a point of saying that he is neither a Nasser nor a Sadat, but whether he intends to be something in between these two or something all his own has remained something of an open question. He has now established himself firmly in power, yet he has not found it necessary or possible to rid the regime of several of the Sadat factions. According to some, the real Mubarak era began only in May 1984, when his political party won the parliamentary elections. Since then, it is maintained, he has been consolidating his *own* regime, in the same low-key style but with firmness and confidence. This new pattern has been revealed on the domestic level in a number of measures, such as the relatively mild sentencing of the members of the Jihad organization in September 1984; the release of the Coptic Patriarch in January 1985; the economic measures passed in 1984 and 1985 aimed at rationalizing the open-door policy through better control and coordination of workers' emigration, foreign currency resources, and imports, exports and investments; and the editorial reshuffles during 1985 in a number of important governmental press organizations.

Some people suspected that certain manifestations of Nasserism were creeping back into the regime as the public sector tried to confront the encroachment of private capital. But most Egyptians probably approved of such measures as the rectification of some of the excesses that had characterized the later Sadat years, and most were – and still are – happy that there was more freedom of expression throughout the country than had existed for a long time. In 1985, for instance, one of the few remaining bans was lifted – that which had affected the publication of *Autumn of Fury*, the controversial book about the legacy of Sadat by the influential writer Muhammad Hasanain Haikal.

Yet this sense of self-confidence should not be allowed to disguise the real difficulties and problems, some of which have been increasing since the mid-1980s.

Economic problems remain as critical as ever, forcing the government to introduce several retrenchment measures in the state budget. The uncertainty over oil prices makes petroleum a relatively unreliable source of income even for the purposes of short-term planning (oil income was £E1,016.8 million in the 1983–4 budget). Government subsidies on basic goods represent a huge drain on the budget: £E1,686 million, or more than one-third of the total budgetary deficit of £E5,012 million in 1983–4.

Tampering with these subsidies has, however, proved politically dangerous. The removal of some of them in January 1977 led to nationwide food riots, while the doubling of the price of bread in September 1984 resulted in violent rioting in the industrial delta town of Kafr al-Dawwar. Eighty-nine arrests were made following the Kafr al-Dawwar events. Significantly, those arrested included seven members of the Nationalist Progressive Unionist Party (a legal left-wing political party) who were accused of publishing articles encouraging workers to revolt. This was one of the few times that the government had arrested members of a legally authorized party using the emergency law that was renewed – after a certain amount of manoeuvring in Parliament – in September 1984. In justifying the renewal of the law, the government emphasized that it would be used only against illegal subversive elements, hinting specifically at the militant Islamic movements.

Mubarak's job was never going to be an easy one, since he needed to deal simultaneously with the economic crisis and with the Islamic radicals. Many thought that it would be risky indeed if he were to follow Sadat's example and neglect these two major challenges under the misguided belief that the tiny Egyptian Left represented the main threat to the regime. In fact, on the same day that the emergency law was renewed, the Supreme Court for State Security finally pronounced its verdict in the case against the Jihad organization for its involvement in Sadat's assassination. Terms of life imprisonment and other prison sentences, but no executions, were given to 110 of the accused, while 190 were found not guilty.

More difficult still is the question of how to deal with the social problems engendered by *infitah*, such as income inequality and cultural alienation (see Chapter 2), which are likely to be at the heart of much potential political unrest. The coexistence of a large public sector and a sizeable private sector means a salary ratio that can be as high as 1 to 50. The contradictions are more stunning when the impact of corruption and speculation is added to the picture. The daily income of some of those who stood trial under Mubarak for illicit dealings was equivalent to the total salary of a university professor during his entire career! Given such inequities, many people believe that Mubarak brought his anti-corruption campaign to a close too soon.

Inflation (ranging between 20% and 30% per annum in the mid-1980s), impossible housing costs (for example, 'key money' for a rented apartment can be equivalent to a university graduate's total salary for ten years) and a high rate of manifest unemployment (about 20%, although nearly one-third of the labour force is working abroad), all contribute to deprivation and frustration, not only among the lower classes but – what is more politically dangerous – among the middle classes as well.

Problems are thus escalating seriously, and this is causing some people to wonder whether a more assertive style of leadership is not required at this stage. Several times the corruption trials have been slowed down, and measures to regulate the economy have been withdrawn; several times the President has appeared not to complete the course he had started to follow; often he gives contradictory signals. The Sadatist network appears to be playing on his fears, and he frequently seems to end up with his 'heart' on one side and the ruler's natural instinct for survival on the other. In many of his acts he is reduced to the role of principal arbiter among competing forces, and the question is often asked, playing on the similarity between the two words, when it will be that he will turn from being a *hakam* (arbiter) into being a *hākim* (ruler)!

The state and the commercial bourgeoisie

In the context of 'rationalizing the open-door economic policy', as its slogan ran, Mubarak's government tried in early 1985 to fight the 'foreign currency and importation mafia', which encompassed not only powerful merchants but also important banking and government officials, some of whom were already on trial. This grouping was believed to be behind the siphoning away from the official economy of the major part of workers' remittances from abroad, estimated at some $3 billion a year. From January 1985 the Egyptian pound was to some extent floated against other currencies (US$1 = £E1.245). For purposes of importation, however, it was made impossible (contrary to the situation pertaining from 1973, when such importations were permitted) to use one's own foreign currency resources directly for the import of goods. All imports would have to be financed through the banking system, which would supply importers with their requirements for foreign currencies at the rates decided on a daily basis by the Central Bank. (The government maintained that this would be done according to market considerations, although critics suspected a heavy bureaucratic touch.) All dealings in foreign currencies outside the banking system were forbidden, and the importation of over 300 items that had local equivalents was subjected to a stricter licensing system.

The government was therefore combining in one package a new foreign-exchange system with a new imports policy. The final touches were also put to a new export-promotion policy, which emphasized such items as textiles, furniture and books. Observers could see that several groups were likely to resist these new arrangements, and that the government's battle against the 'parallel economy' would by no means be easy. But had it succeeded, it would probably have gone a reasonable way towards reducing the then existing imbalance between imports (£E9.5 billion) and exports (£E4.5 billion), which was perhaps the most urgent of Egypt's economic problems at that point. However, these economic measures immediately became the subject of controversy among three competing groups: (a) a state bourgeoisie represented by the public-sector managers and technocrats; (b) an embryonic private-sector entrepreneurial class interested in all profitable investment opportunities; and (c) a parasitic economic mafia of currency dealers and speculators, monopoly importers and smugglers, black marketeers, and so on.

The last of these groupings had been hit particularly hard by the currency and importation measures of 1985; it was believed to include several hundred currency dealers (including seven 'giants') and some 2,000 importers (including 20 'giants'), and was estimated by some to deal in at least $6 billion a year. These people have very strong links and support within the commercial banking system, virtually dominating the Islamic banks and investment companies, and have established a powerful network of bureaucratic and mass media contacts.[10] They used all manner of tactics to resist the currency and importation measures – spreading rumours that these measures were the work of the Minister of the Economy alone and not of the whole government, and temporarily halting their import-ing activities in order to create an atmosphere of shortages and uncertainties that would force a revoking of the measures. *Al-Wafd* newspaper was especially vociferous in attacking both the economic regulations and the Minister of the Economy, and stiff pressure was put on the government to revoke the decisions by the Federation of Chambers of Commerce, the Federation of Industries and, most particularly, the Egyptian Businessmen's Association.[11] Thus, for some months an economic war was waged between a government that appeared to be trying to accumulate and administer sufficient foreign exchange to meet, in a balanced way, the legitimate require-ments of the public and the private sector, and a 'currency and importation mafia' which, by creating shortages and bottlenecks, was able to claim that there was no solution to Egypt's economic problems without its services.

The finance and business lobby ended the victors, with the resignation/dismissal of Dr Mustafa al-Sa'id, the Minister of the Economy, over policy issues as well as alleged personal scandals. A new minister replaced him, and the 'January Decrees' that had aroused the anger of the mercantile lobby and the foreign banks were hurriedly succeeded by the 'April Decrees'.[12] Once again the importers could bring in goods directly, relying on their own foreign currency resources (usually acquired on the black market) and without channelling their operations through the legal banking system.

Since the January Decrees were applied for barely three months, it is pointless to speak, as some did, about their lack of effectiveness. What is important is that the main policy issues behind these decrees and counter-decrees have not died away, and will not do so for some time to come, since the conflict between the developmentalists on the one hand and the commercial/financial lobby on the other is likely to continue.

In May 1987, following negotiations with the International Monetary Fund (IMF), major monetary reforms were announced, aimed at floating the Egyptian pound and enforcing state control over the foreign-exchange market through the formal banking system. Several meetings were held with managers of the private banks to enlist their cooperation. It is not clear at the time of writing (August 1987) whether the government will manage this time to gain the upper hand over the commercial/financial lobby, but there are signs of resistance from the very wealthy Islamic banks and 'Companies for the Employment of Monies in the Islamic Way'.

The state and the Islamic militants
Most observers suspected that Sadat was behind the initial revival of the militant Islamic groups, his assumption being that this would help to counterbalance the political weight of Nasserists and socialists. But these groups were soon to acquire an independent life and logic of their own, so that by 1977 they felt strong enough to start to challenge the government directly. Sadat appeared to have realized their potential danger only in mid-1981, by which time it was too late to stop them. Their activities subsided for a number of years following his assassination and the subsequent trials, but it is generally thought that membership of the movements did not decline substantially. Government sources believe that there are over twenty such groups, the most significant of which are al-Jihad (Holy Struggle, believed to have been behind the killing of Sadat) and al-Takfir w'al-Hijra (Excommunication and Emigration, which was responsible for the murder of an ex-Minister of Religious Affairs in 1977).[13]

Although members of the team directly involved in Sadat's assassination were tried and executed shortly after the event, members of the larger group behind the affair were sentenced only three years later. The fact that the announcement of the court's verdict was postponed several times probably indicates just how uncomfortable the regime is in dealing with these groups. Although a majority of Egyptians seems to condemn political violence, large segments of the population sympathize with many of the sentiments and the zeal of the Islamic youth.

One of the most difficult political tests for the regime will always be how to keep the militant Islamic movements under control without wrecking the entire democratic experiment, as Sadat managed to do shortly before his assassination when he arrested large numbers of political activists throughout Egypt.

Some people believe that had these groups not brought about their own temporary downfall by killing Sadat, a more serious Islamic revolution, not unlike that of Iran, might well have taken place in Egypt sooner or later. Although such movements are not at present strong enough to seize political power, they seem to be capable of challenging and destabilizing the existing order. Most analysts agree that the challenge of such groups cannot be removed unless something radical is done to solve the socio-economic problems of the recently urbanized and formally educated youth, from among whom the militant religious movements tend to draw their cadres.[14] For example, the student demonstrations that took place in three Egyptian universities in November and December 1984, including for the first time particularly violent riots in the usually quiescent university of al-Azhar, served as a reminder that the grievances and anxieties of Egyptian young people are still as serious as ever, and that – given the limited possibilities for political participation available to them – they are more than likely to find an outlet in politicized religion.

The apprehensions of the Mubarak regime were particularly aroused from 1985 onwards by the apparent escalation of fundamentalist opposition. There has been a constant arm-twisting by a large following of fundamentalists, led by Shaikh Hafez Salama, to force the government to announce the immediate application of *shari'a* (Islamic law). Shaikh Salama, the preacher at the famous al-Nūr mosque in Cairo, first appeared in the national limelight during the Arab-Israeli war in 1973, as a leader of popular resistance in Suez. He came to political prominence again in summer 1985 with his preparations for a huge march, in which participants were going to walk all the way from the al-Nūr mosque to the President's residence to demand the immediate application of religious laws. A hasty decree issued by the Interior Minister prevented this potentially threatening demonstration from going ahead.

The government, however, used the occasion to announce, in a pre-emptive act, that all mosques in the country (whether government- or privately-sponsored) would be subject to the jurisdiction and supervision of the Ministry of Awqaf (Endowments and Religious Affairs), including the right of approving the appointment of preachers. At the same time, the government authorities and the ruling party's members of parliament continued with the official line that the application of *shari'a* was accepted in principle but that its enforcement should take place in a gradual and 'scientific' manner. Many people realize, however, that, given the limited success of the government in solving the complex socio-economic problems of the country (especially those affecting the urban youth), and the continuing refusal by the authorities to grant political party status to the movements that most express the grievances of young people (e.g. the Muslim Brothers and the Nasserists), there will be little alternative for such people but to take their grievances to the streets.

There are no signs so far that political Islam has burrowed its way deeply into either the working class or the armed forces, or among those at the very bottom of the social ladder, the lumpenproletariat. Its chances of success are likely to be highest among the last of these three groups. And of course the urban lumpenproletariat is also amenable to the influence of the merchant-artisan class (i.e. the *bazaaris*), which is being increasingly attracted to political Islam and has a history of involvement in certain violent activities. Above all, the lack of dynamic political participation is a serious problem, since it forces many young people in the direction of the radical Islamic movements. Although these movements are still small and isolated, their determination is beyond doubt, and there are already signs – at least with regard to the Jihad organization – that they may have broken loose from the closed circle of students into a broader community of clerks, artisans, merchants, preachers, officials and soldiers.[15] Their main handicap, possibly, is that they have not offered the ordinary citizen a *solution* for his nagging daily problems of surviving and living. However, they have presented an *alternative* domain of concern over morality, ethics and family life: if the economic problem cannot be solved, why not try to achieve superiority by being morally pure!

The state and political parties

As already noted, demands for increased political participation have been building up for some time. In response, 'platforms' (*manabir*) were allowed to adopt distinctive programmes and produce lists for parliamentary elections in 1976. Shortly afterwards, the 'platform' organizations were allowed to turn themselves into legal political parties. However, both the 1976 and the 1979 parliamentary elections gave the government party a very substantial majority in the legislative branch. At present the legislature is centred on a People's Assembly, Majlis al-Sha'b, made up of 448 elected members and 10 appointed members. But parallel to it is a Consultative Council, Majlis al-Shura, having 140 elected members and 70 by appointment.

The first parliamentary elections under Mubarak were held in May 1984 under a rather curious new electoral law based on proportional representation. According to this law, which is still applicable, no parties are allowed representation in parliament unless they obtain at least 8% of all national votes (this meant some 423,000 votes in the 1984 elections). All votes (and seats) acquired by those political parties that do not reach the required percentage are added automatically to those of the winning party, which also monopolizes the 30 seats reserved exclusively for women in the People's Assembly. (This provision, concerning women's representation, was cancelled in the 1987 elections.) Applying these regulations to the 1984 elections, the ruling National Democratic Party (NDP) achieved 72.9% of votes and 87% of the seats in the People's Assembly; the right-wing New Wafd Party (NWP), 15% of votes and 13% of seats; the Socialist Labour Party (SLP), 7.1% of votes and no seats; the left-wing Nationalist Progressive Unionist Rally Party (NPURP), 4.2% of votes and no seats; and the Liberal Socialist Party (LSP), 0.65% of votes and no seats. (See Table 4.1 at the end of the chapter.)

The elections made it clear, therefore, that the ruling party, headed by Mubarak himself, was well in control. But the extent to which this 'control' was actually responsible for the results of the elections remained controversial for quite some time. What was obvious was that the ruling party fared much better in the countryside, where the government's grip over local government and the security machine is tighter. The opposition, by contrast, registered impressive support in the large cities, gaining 38.4% of all votes in Cairo, 32.7% in Alexandria, 36% in Suez and as much as 53.3% of all votes in Port Said.[16]

All in all, however, it appeared that the government had managed to marginalize the existing opposition parties, with the possible exception of the pre-revolutionary Wafd Party (which succeeded not only in legalizing itself as a result of winning a judicial case against the government, but also in winning a reasonable number of seats in a tight election through alliance with the Muslim Brothers). It is possible that the country might indeed have been settling for a *de facto* one-party system (similar to that in Mexico), especially since it remains extremely difficult for new parties to be formed under the existing 'Parties Law'. Yet, by persecuting the small parties, the government might inadvertently have helped to promote the idea of electoral alliances: first between the Muslim Brothers and the Wafd, then between the Muslim Brothers and Labour/Liberals.

As expected, the elections in April 1987 saw the NDP victorious again, although with fewer seats than in the 1984 elections. Of over 14 million registered voters, less than half actually voted. According to the rules, any party not obtaining in these elections some 546,000 votes nationally would lose any seats gained locally. The NDP received about 4,752,000 votes (69.6%); all opposition parties together obtained about 2,073,000 votes, of which about 1,164,000 (17%) went to the alliance of Labour (SLP)/Liberal (LSP) with the Ikhwan (Muslim Brothers), about 746,000 (10.9%) to the Wafd, some 151,000 (2.21%) to the NPURP and about 13,000 (0.19%) to the minor religious party al-Umma. These party votes translated into the following seats (excluding the 48 seats specifically allocated for 'independents'): 309 to the NDP, 56 to the alliance of Labour/Liberal with the Ikhwan and 35 to the Wafd; the NPURP and the Umma Party had no seats. Of the seats reserved for the 'independents', 40 also went to candidates sponsored by the NDP. (See Table 4.2.)

It should be observed, however, that the NDP's share of seats in this election was 80 fewer than in the 1984 election (or 40 if one counts independents supported by the NDP), while the opposition's share increased by at least 30 seats. But instead of the Wafd, which formed the main opposition party in the 1984 parliament, the main opposition block is now represented by the alliance between the nationalist-Islamist Labour Party, the right-wing Liberal Party and the fundamentalist Ikhwan. This means that the Ikhwan, although still technically an illegal organization, will now be substantially represented in the parliament (and by some of its most distinguished leaders) for the first time since the revolution of 1952. The Wafd's ageing and paternalistic leadership, its wavering over secularism and temporary alliance with Ikhwan, and its obsessive hatred of Nasser appear to have reduced its popularity.

The government party has thus won again, even though there have been repeated accusations of rigging and corruption, most notably from the leader of the Wafd Party, who described the election as 'the largest forgery of the people's will and a lasting stain on the forehead of the present era'.[17] But even without much open rigging and corruption (although in this case there were violent skirmishes involving governmental and security officials in the working-class town of Kafr al-Dawwar and elsewhere), the NDP has access to a whole organizational network, especially in the countryside, that ensures that there are proportionately more votes cast in the countryside, and that these votes go in the desired direction. As with the 1984 elections, the highest turnout was in the countryside, while in Cairo the turnout was estimated at only 20%. One would presume that those who were inclined not to support the government party found it easier to 'vote with their feet' in Cairo than did their counterparts in the smaller towns and in the villages, who live in the tight grip of a control-oriented local-government system introduced by Sadat in 1979. The government operates a patronage system in the localities whereby public services and economic privileges are identified with the NDP. At the same time, most local officials, including regional governors, tend to identify themselves with the ruling party. As one governor put it bluntly: 'I support the NDP; for the governor is, in the first and last resort, partisan. A success for the NDP signifies a people that is behind its leader and which supports his steps.'[18]

It remains to be seen whether, confident again of its control over political life, the regime will be prepared to allow parties freer scope for activity, or whether whatever limited competition existed in the 1987 elections will play on the leadership's fears and apprehensions. Shortly after the elections, there were unconfirmed reports that

President Mubarak was getting rather impatient with the parties. He is said to have criticized their attempts at contrasting the 'government' with the 'people' and to have condemned their exploitation of the 'religious surge'. Reportedly he went so far as to suggest that there were no real political parties in Egypt (the NDP not excluded), just a few opposition leaders and newspapers. He was also said to be reconsidering the system of election by party lists and thinking of reintroducing the system based on electing individuals.[19]

The main question, therefore, is whether the regime is prepared to allow competing forces the chance of coming to power democratically, or whether – in a time of mounting tension – it is more likely, as one analyst predicted, 'to contract rather than to expand the scope of participation'.[20]

Public order and the role of the military

As we have seen, Egypt's problems are reaching a critical point, at which simply muddling through may no longer be a sufficient response. The year 1986 was particularly ominous. It started in February with the mutiny of 17,000–20,000 members of the Central Security Forces (CSF), a paramilitary leviathan of some 300,000 personnel, consisting largely of conscripts rejected by the army for their uncouthness and illiteracy. CSF members serve for a period of three years, during which time they are consistently humiliated and exploited by their officers, and used either for protecting the main symbols of indulgence and decadence (both domestic and foreign), or for quelling the demonstrations of students and workers, whose discontent must frequently appear to them justified. Supposed technically to be doing their national service, CSF conscripts are paid a mere £E6.00 a month, barely enough to buy cigarettes, let alone to support their wives and families.

It is not surprising in such circumstances that the news about a possible extension of their service met with a violent response,[21] much as the news of price rises had precipitated the food riots of January 1977.[22] The CSF riots were themselves 'food riots' of sorts – a 'slaves' revolt', as some have expressed it. If the January 1977 events represented in their final stages the revolt of an urban dispossessed against the early bitter harvest of *infitah*, then the 1986 events should be looked at as a revolt by the lowest-level state-servants against the core of the state, at a stage when the later bitter harvest of *infitah* had come in. For the CSF recruits had come from the lowest classes in some of the most remote and neglected parts of the countryside, at a time when income differentials had reached extremes not seen since pre-revolutionary times. It was mainly the unpopularity of the CSF and the intervention of the army that made the containment of the revolt possible, although not without heavy losses of life and property. As in 1977, the armed forces were called in to restore order, doubtless adding to the power of a military establishment whose growing professionalization since 1967 does not imply a minimal socio-economic or political role.

The same year – 1986 – also saw an escalation of acts of violence by militant Islamic groups, including mysterious fires and explosions in Cairo and several Upper Egyptian towns, which carried on well into 1987, and the announcement by the government for the first time that one of these organizations, intent on overthrowing the government and establishing an Islamic order, had a number of army officers among its founders. Workers' strikes occurred throughout the year, including most notably – in terms of its impact on the general public – the well-organized strike by train drivers, which resulted in the government disbanding their syndicate and putting a few of their members to the State Security Parquet.

The years 1986 and 1987 also witnessed some of the toughest negotiations with the United States and the International Monetary Fund at a time of escalating financial and economic crisis. Foreign policy issues of this kind have important domestic repercussions in political and class terms, for there are those who cannot wait to wield the IMF 'stick' against the already impoverished masses. 'Rationalization measures' are often another term for austerity as far as the poor are concerned, and it is always easier for the state to take from those within administrative reach, rather than from the wealthy. Nor can anyone determine at what point the ordinary Egyptian citizen will lose his proverbial patience and eternal smile and take to the streets in protest against what he would regard as patently unjust raising of prices and removal of subsidies.

By mid-1987, furthermore, attempts at political assassination appeared to be escalating. These included the attack outside his house on Hasan Abu-Basha, ex-Minister of the Interior, who was held by Islamic militants to be responsible for torturing their leaders (the fundamentalist Jihad organization claimed responsibility), and the attempted murder of two American diplomats on their way to the US embassy (for which responsibility was claimed by a little-known 'Egyptian Revolution' organization, previously involved in attempted assassinations of Israeli officials in 1984, 1985 and 1986). There was also an attempt to assassinate Makram Muhammad Ahmad, editor of *al-Musawar* magazine, who had written articles calling for tighter measures against the two 'terrorist centres' that existed in Egypt: one, the militant Islamic fundamentalist grouping; and the other, radical, anti-American and anti-Israeli.

As the events of the food riots of 1977 and the mutiny of the security forces in 1986 have shown, the Egyptian army is the last-resort keeper of order and, therefore, the ultimate guarantor of the existing political regime. Some analysts would even claim that it is the major institution of power in Egypt, lying at the heart of the country's political process.[23]

Although the Egyptian government has been almost completely 'civilianized',[24] President Mubarak, like Nasser and Sadat before him, is by origin a military man. The Egyptian army retrieved its professionalism after the 1967 war and regained its 'honour' in the war of October 1973. To emphasize political neutrality, the armed forces are no longer corporate members of the Alliance of the Working Forces of the People, as they were under Nasser, and military men are not permitted to join political parties or to vote in elections. However, the foreign policy orientation of the army was reversed under Sadat,[25] and since the 1979 peace treaty the armed forces have become increasingly involved in domestic developmental and economic activities.[26] This keeps a still large army busy, and gives it access – like the rest of the government establishment – to the symbiotic linkage-points between the public and the private sectors. Pay and other working conditions have also improved.

In both 1977 and 1986, when the army was called upon to restore public order, it showed little interest in taking political power into its own hands. If the armed forces were to develop any signs of discontent, these would probably be over such professional concerns as quantities, types and sources of armaments, or the existence and strength of alternative paramilitary forces. However, one should not completely rule out other possible sources of tension, such as a growing duality between the army's 'combatant' and its 'economic' wings, or a conflict between the requirements of a pro-Western stance on the one hand and brotherly sentiments towards an Arab people on the other.

Except in the case of a total collapse in public order, the possibility of a direct intervention by the army in politics remains remote. Even so, as the political opposition became more critical of the regime during the mid-1980s, President Mubarak did warn – in a frequently cited press interview – of a 'dangerous alternative' to his rule: this has usually been taken to imply a possible *coup d'état*.[27]

It should also be remembered that, however professional the Egyptian military may be, since it is basically an army of conscripts, it cannot be shielded from political, religious or class issues circulating through society at large (Sadat was, after all, assassinated at a *military* parade). No outsider can estimate to what extent radical Islamic ideologies are finding recruits or sympathizers within the armed forces, but this is certainly a possibility to which any government should keep alert. On the other hand, the armed forces are now so large, diverse and carefully located that any serious attempt to organize a *coup d'état* at a relatively junior level would be bound to require such long and extensive communications that the authorities could hardly fail to notice. A coup by fiat from the top, in the Latin American style, is also quite unlikely.[28]

Prospects for stability

Although the Egyptian political system remains remarkably stable, serious tensions and pressures have been building up since the mid-1970s. As the problems of socio-economic inequality and socio-cultural alienation mount internally, and as the country's dependence on the outside world becomes ever more critical, it is likely that more people will increasingly incline either towards a solution based on political Islam ('cultural authenticity', 'collective morals', etc.), or else towards one that would represent a type of neo-Nasserism (socio-economic planning, an active non-aligned foreign policy, etc.).

Neither the proponents of political Islam nor those of neo-Nasserism, however, are organizationally capable of taking power on their own. If, therefore, a change in the existing order is ever to take place, it will have to be achieved through intervention by the military. Such an intervention would most probably take place on the occasion of an acute social and/or political crisis, accompanied by widespread acts of violence.

As has already been pointed out, the potential for political violence is ever present in Egypt's existing situation of high social tension. In the last decade, such violence has tended to express itself in one of the following forms:

(a) food riots, especially among the urban masses, such as those of 1977 and the lesser ones of 1984;

(b) workers' (illegal) strikes, especially in the large public-sector factories of Helwan, Mahalla al-Kubra and Kafr al-Dawwar, such as those that occurred in 1974, 1975, 1976, 1984, 1986 and 1987; and

(c) sectarian conflicts between Muslims and Christians, and/or 'terrorist acts' by members of the militant Islamic organizations, such as those of 1974, 1977, 1981, 1986 and 1987.

The regime has so far been lucky in that these three varieties of violence – urban, industrial and religious – have taken place separately and in isolation from each other; it would be a different matter if such expressions of political unrest were to occur simultaneously. The CSF rebellion of 1986 lies somewhere in between type (a) and type (b) in that it was a 'food riot' of sorts but was launched by a manner of 'state worker/servant'. The mutiny could have sparked off a much more serious popular movement had it not been for the unpopularity of the CSF.

The regime, rather than attempting structural reform, has responded to such crises on the basis of immediate, but limited, confrontation. The crisis is dealt with as a passing occurrence, a separate, self-contained event. Its immediate igniting spark is taken as the cause, and not simply as the symptom of a more problematic situation. The main treatment has been summarized by one analyst as 'subsidies for the masses and selective imprisonment for potentially dangerous leaders'. Yet, he continues, 'this type of political stabilization leads to dangerous instability.'[29]

Forecasting doomsday is a risky and unpleasant task, but if a worst-case scenario for extra-constitutional change is to be imagined,[30] its elements and conjunctures would go something like this:

– some genuine economic grievances and/or nationalist concerns would arouse the workers and/or the students into organized protest (demonstrations, strikes, etc.);

– militant Islamic elements from among the students and/or the artisan/merchant community would then give the movement Islamic slogans and impart a religious flavour to it;

– attempts by the security forces to disperse the gatherings would lead to their diffusion among the urban masses: elements among the latter would then attack symbols of state authority, economic luxury and 'social decadence';
– urban chaos would ensue: arson, theft, thuggery and destruction, possibly for days; and
– the only possible saviour would appear to be the armed forces, which would eventually restore law and order in support of the civilian government, as they did in 1977 and 1986.

Yet although still unlikely, no one can completely rule out the remote possibility – in such an intense crisis situation – of a military group trying to impose its political preferences. Such a group might be on the side of law and order, or it might be motivated mainly by professional concerns, or it might be tempted by, or sympathetic to, the so-called 'Islamic alternative'. The end-result of this last variant of the worst-case scenario (and still the least likely to happen, to judge by existing realities) would be either a coup with Islamic leanings, or else – even more unlikely – a series of events that would eventually lead to a full-fledged 'Islamic revolution'. This last is a very alarming scenario indeed, but one which must be turning over, frighteningly, in the minds of many Egyptians.

Conclusion
What is to be done? There is no immediate magic solution to Egypt's problems, especially in the economic sphere. Things can be ameliorated and rationalized here and there, and more encouragement can be given to productive activities, especially to industry, which represents the only economic hope for a fast-growing population in a country with very little arable land. But Egypt cannot become a prosperous society overnight. The only way of preventing the hard economic situation from leading to a political explosion is to involve people more closely in the problems, and in the process of *trying* to solve them. In other words, until the escalating socio-economic problems can be solved, 'democratization' will remain the only possible outlet for avoiding a serious crisis.

Democratization, in this context, should mean (in addition to freedom of expression, which does, to a large extent, exist) the right of assembly, including demonstrations and strikes, and the right to form political parties. A party system under which the Nasserists or the Muslim Brothers are not allowed to form parties is not a party system. Not that allowing these two political forces to form political parties would automatically mean their ascent to power. The Ikhwan could lose much of its mystique if it came into the open and were obliged to offer practical solutions for real, everyday problems; similarly, the Nasserists might fail to reconcile their ranks and cliques and to agree on a common ideology and acceptable leadership. However, most people would agree that an eventual ascent to power by a constitutional Islamic or Nasserist political party that had won its case popularly and democratically is a much better prospect than if either group came to power through a violent military coup or a sweeping religious revolution.

Furthermore, compared with the relatively little that the regime can do to make immediate improvements in Egypt's economic and international situation, the area of democratization lies wide open, and therefore offers good chances of success. Significant progress has already been made in this respect, but there is popular demand for more. It is in democratization, therefore, that Mubarak's real contribution could lie.

Notes

1 See A. Abdel-Malek, *Egypt: Military Society* (New York: Random House, 1968); R.H. Dekmejian, *Egypt under Nasir* (New York: SUNY Press, 1971); N.N. Ayubi, *Bureaucracy and Politics in Contemporary Egypt* (London: Ithaca Press, 1980).

2 Compare: Mark Cooper, *The Transformation of Egypt* (London: Croom Helm, 1982); John Waterbury, *The Egypt of Nasser and Sadat* (Princeton, N.J.: Princeton U.P., 1983); Raymond Hinnebusch, *Egyptian Politics under Sadat* (New York: Cambridge U.P., 1985).

3 Compare: Mourad M. Wahba, 'The Role of the State in the Egyptian Economy: 1945–1981', unpublished D.Phil. thesis, Oxford University, 1986.

4 See also Nadia Ramsis Farah, 'Development and the Crisis of Political Transformation' [in Arabic], in *al-Manar*, June 1985, pp. 42–69.

5 See N.N. Ayubi, 'Implementation Capability and Political Feasibility of the Open Door Policy in Egypt', in M.H. Kerr and E.S. Yassin, eds., *Rich and Poor States in the Middle East* (Boulder, Colo.: Westview Press, 1982); Samia Sa'id Imam, 'Al-Usul al-ijtima'iyya li

nukhbat al-infitah' [Social Origins of the Infitah Elite], unpublished M.Sc. thesis, Cairo University, Faculty of Economics and Political Science, 1986.

6 The state employed some 5 million people in 1987, of whom 3.4 million were in the civil service and 1.6 million were in the public sector, their total wages and salaries accounting for about £E8,000m.

7 'Adil Ghunaim, *Al-namudhaj al-misri li-ra'simaliyya al-dawla al-tabi'a* [The Egyptian Model of Dependent State Capitalism], (Cairo: Dar al-Mustaqbal al-'Arabi, 1986).

8 Compare: 'Ismat Saifuddawla, *Al-Istibdad al-dimuqrati* [Democratic Despotism], (Cairo: Dar al-Mustaqbal al-'Arabi, 1983), pp. 127–69.

9 R.H. Dekmejian, 'Government and Politics', in R.F. Nyrop, ed., *Egypt: A Country Study* (Washington, D.C.: American University, 1983), p. 200.

10 For details, see A. Ghunaim (1986) and S. Imam (1986).

11 Centre for Political and Strategic Studies, *Al-Taqrir al-istratiji al-'Arabi* [The Arab Strategic Report for 1985], (Cairo: CPSS, 1986), p. 340–2.

12 These developments are well covered in *al-Ahram al-Iqtisadi*, January to April 1985.

13 See N.N. Ayubi, 'The Political Revival of Islam: The Case of Egypt', *International Journal of Middle East Studies*, vol. 12 (1980), no. 4; and Ayubi, 'The Politics of Militant Islamic Groups in the Middle East', *Journal of International Affairs*, vol. 36, no. 2, pp. 982–3.

14 See H.N. Ansari, 'The Islamic Militants in Egyptian Politics', *International Journal of Middle East Studies*, vol. 16 (1984), no. 9, pp. 130ff.

15 G. Kepel, *The Prophet and Pharaoh: Muslim Extremism in Egypt*, trans. (London: Al-Saqi, 1985), pp. 216–17 and map p. 22.

16 All election figures throughout this study are derived from official data as published in the national press of Egypt.

17 *Al-Wafd*, 8 April 1987.

18 Quoted in A. Hilal, M.K. Al-Sayyid and I. Badruddin, *Tajribat al-dimuqratiyya fi misr* [The Democratic Experience in Egypt, 1970–1981], (Cairo: Al-Markaz al-'Arabi, 1982).

19 This was mentioned by President Mubarak in his speech to leading press editors and journalists on 4 June 1987, as reported by *Al-Tadamun* (the London-based Arabic magazine), 13 June 1987. Official sources, however, denied some of the reported contents of this speech (see, e.g., *al-Ahram*, 16 June 1987).

20 Friedmann Büttner, 'A Country Scenario Analysis of Egypt', *Viertel Jahres Berichte*, no. 96 (June 1984), pp. 163–79.

21 The events of February 1986 were candidly covered by the Egyptian press. This analysis is based on extensive readings in the government and opposition press of that period.

22 The events of 18 and 19 January 1977 are complex. Yet in spite of their importance, there is hardly any literature available on them, with the exception of one recent book which fortunately is documented with a variety of material, including the text of the court verdict on the case (which, incidentally, shows the Egyptian judiciary still to be the protector of human and individual rights in the country). The stages through which the January 1977 events passed are important to distinguish, since they are likely to be repeated in similar occurrences of urban protest. (i) The protest starts among the public-sector industrial proletariat and/or university students, with specific slogans and clear demands. (ii) As the protesters move to the main city squares, they are joined by other workers, students, officials, artisans, merchants, etc. However, they are still quite orderly and their demands remain clear. But it is usually at this stage that security forces intervene and disperse the crowds with violence, whereupon the crowds respond with counter-violence. (iii) As confrontation develops, confusion erupts and the escaping crowds take to smaller squares and side streets. At this point, the movement seems to be taken over by stray elements of the lumpenproletariat (and excited teenagers), and mounting acts of destruction, arson and theft take place. For details on the 1977 riots, see Husain 'Abd al-Raziq, *Misr fi 18 & 19 yanayir* [Egypt on 18 and 19 January 1977: A Political Documentary Study], (Cairo: Dar Shahid, 1985).

23 Sa'd Zahran, *Fi usul al-siyasa al-misriyya* [On the Essentials of Egyptian Politics], (Cairo: Dar al-Mustaqbal al-'Arabi, 1985), pp. 190–1.

24 Cf. 'Abd al-Ghaffar Rashad, 'Al-Nukhba al-siyasiyya' [The Political Elite], in A. Hilal, ed., *Al-Nizam al-Siyasi* [The Political System of Egypt], (Cairo: Al-Markaz al-'Arabi, 1983), pp. 108–18.

25 Dekmejian, *op.cit.*, p. 203.

26 These activities include building roads and railways, bridges, irrigation channels and water pipes, transport and communication networks, and a wide variety of factories, laboratories, clinics and training centres. They have also included setting up a large bakery complex and other 'food security projects' and have even extended to making the arrangements for performances of *Aida* at the Pyramids. Such expansion by the armed forces into civilian activities has been controversial. See Centre for Political and Strategic Studies, *op.cit.* (as note 11), pp. 425–9.

27 See, for example, *al-Mustaqbal*, 8 March 1986, and *Guardian*, 8 April 1986.

28 For an interesting discussion of this point, see Büttner, *op.cit.*, p. 176.

29 *Ibid.*, p. 173.

30 Compare Scenario II and Scenario III in Malcolm Kerr, 'Egypt and
the Arabs in the Future: Some Scenarios', in M.H. Kerr and E.S.
Yassin, eds., *Rich and Poor States in the Middle East*, pp. 449–72.

Tables

Table 4.1 The main political parties, 1987*

Party	History	Composition
National Democratic Party (NDP)	Partly successor to the Arab Socialist Union (1963), but more directly to the Centre Platform [Egypt Arab Socialist Organization] (1976), turned party (1977), and renamed NDP (1987). New name is meant to imply continuity with the pre-revolutionary (1907) Nationalist Party led by the nationalist-traditionalist patriot Mustafa Kamil.	Officials, functionaries, technocrats and, increasingly, traders, contractors, rural magnates, etc. The establishment party. Headed by Sadat, then by Mubarak. Organs: *Mayo* (but also much of the national press); *Al-Liwa' al-Islami*; *Shabab Biladi*.
Liberal Socialist Party (LSP)	Successor to the Right Platform (1976).	Supposed to represent the 'National bourgeoisie'. Headed by an ex-Free Officer in support of free enterprise (Mustafa Kamil Murad). Organ: *Al-Ahrar*.
Nationalist Progressive Unionist Rally Party (Tajammu', NPURP)	Successor to the Left Platform (1976).	Intellectuals, employees, technocrats, workers. Alliance between some Marxists (there is also an underground Egyptian Communist Party), some Nasserists (others seeking separate party), and a few progressive religious scholars. Headed by a Marxist ex-Free Officer (Khalid Muhyi al-Din), supports public sector, non-alignment. Organ: *Al-Ahali*.

(continues overleaf)

Table 4.1 (*concluded*)

Party	History	Composition
Socialist Labour Party (SLP)	Created by Sadat (1978) to represent a tame opposition, but acquired momentum of its own. Represents to some extent continuation of the pre-revolutionary and populist-Islamist Young Egypt Party (1933), also known as the Socialist Party.	Headed by an ex-member of a Sadat cabinet who used to be a cadre of Young Egypt. Grew increasingly oppositional, and populist-Islamist in orientation. Opposes peace treaty with Israel. Head is Ibrahim Shukri. Organ: *Al-Sha'b*.
New Wafd Party (NWP)	Formed in 1978, but soon dissolved itself in protest, to re-emerge in 1984. Continuation of the pre-revolutionary secular reformist party of Egyptian nationalism, the Egyptian Wafd Party (1918).	Continuation of the right-wing branch of the old Wafd. Presents itself as the party of individual freedom and 'true' capitalism. Membership mainly officials, professionals and lawyers, and only a few businessmen. Strongly anti-Nasserist. Headed (for life) by the Old Wafd leader Fu'ad Siraj al-Din. Organ: *Al-Wafd*.
Umma Party	Established 1984.	Tiny Islamist party. Headed by Ahmad al-Sabahi. Organ: *Al-Umma*.
Al-Ikhwan al-Muslimun (Muslim Brotherhood)	Founded as a movement (1927), became increasingly involved in politics, and suffered several crises before the 1952 revolution and two further crises under Nasser (1954 and 1965/6). Under Sadat was allowed to publish but not to organize formally. Still technically not legal, but submitting candidates for elections on the Wafd list in 1984 and on the Labour list in 1987.	A fundamentalist movement based on political Islam, calling for the full application of *shari'a*. Membership is mainly lower-middle class but also artisans, teachers, officials, merchants, and university graduates. Headed by Hamid Abu Al-Nasr. Other militant Islamic societies (e.g. al-Jihad) may be loosely affiliated with the Ikhwan. Organs: *Al-Da'wa*; *Al-I'tisam* (both suspended in September 1981).

*The Ikhwan has been included in the list, although technically it is not a legalized political party.

Table 4.2 Elections to the People's Assembly

OCTOBER AND NOVEMBER 1976

Platforms	*Seats*
Arab Socialist Organization	280
Liberal Socialist Organization	12
Nationalist Progressive Unionist Rally	2
Independents	48
Nominated by President	10
Vacant and filled by subsequent by-elections	8
	—
Total	360

JUNE 1979

Party	*Seats*
NDP	330
SLP	29
LSP	3
NPURP	—
Independents	10
Nominated by President	10
Vacant: to be filled by elections	10
	—
Total	392

MAY 1984

Party	*Votes (%)*	*Seats*
NDP	72.9	389
NWP	15.1	59
(incl. M.B.)		(8)
SLP	7.1	—
NPURP	4.2	—
		—
		448
Nominated by President		10
		—
Total		458

(*continues overleaf*)

Table 4.2 (*concluded*)

APRIL 1987

Party	Votes (%)	Seats on party slates	'Independent' seats
NDP	69.6	309	40
SLP (Alliance)	17.0	56	4
(incl. M.B.)		(36)	
NWP	10.9	35	—
NPURP	2.21	—	—
Umma	0.19	—	—
Independents*	—	—	(4)
		400	48
Nominated by President		10	
Total		458	

*Apparently no really independent candidate succeeded; only the ones who were sponsored by existing parties.

5

EXTERNAL RELATIONS

Michael Weir*

The strategic importance of Egypt, situated at the meeting-point of Europe, Africa and Asia, with a coastline on two oceans, has ensured that its rulers and people have seldom been free to enjoy in tranquillity the self-sufficient existence that the extraordinary 'gift of the Nile' could provide. Nowadays, conditioned partly by our European outlook and partly by the language of Egyptian nationalism, we tend to see Egyptian history as a chronicle of invasion and occupation by foreign powers – Persians, Greeks, Romans, Byzantines, Arabs, Turks, down to Napoleon and the British. For the most part, the invaders were ultimately either absorbed into or expelled by the enduring Egyptian body politic. But there were not a few periods in which Egypt played the imperial role itself, under a variety of rulers including the early Pharaohs, Saladin, Muhammad Ali and Nasser. More often than not, their antagonists have been the rulers of the other great river-basin, Mesopotamia, in an unending contest for control over Syria.

In the twentieth century the regional balance has been altered by two unforeseen developments of overwhelming significance, the creation of Israel and the exploitation of the oil resources of the Gulf. Such changes have posed both a challenge and an opportunity for Egypt's post-revolutionary leaders in their common endeavour

*Michael Weir was British Ambassador to Egypt from 1979 to 1985.

79

to reassert, through a dynamic foreign policy, Egypt's historic importance in the Middle East and farther afield.

While the mainstream of the Arab nationalist movement gathered force in the first half of the twentieth century, Egypt stood aside, its politicians more intent on getting rid of the British occupation. But they consistently maintained, if only in rhetoric, Muhammad Ali's claim to the natural leadership of the Arab world. Indeed the foundations of Nasser's pan-Arab policy were laid in 1945, when Nahhas Pasha ousted Nuri Said of Iraq from the leadership of the Arab unity movement and established the Arab League in Cairo, with a largely Egyptian staff. Nasser's outstanding achievement was to exploit the impact of his *coup d'état* to mobilize popular opinion in the Third World behind a bid for Egyptian leadership on an almost global scale. Rationalized in his autobiographical *Philosophy of the Revolution* as a divine mission on behalf of three interconnected circles – Arab, African and Islamic – it was consecrated at the Bandung Conference of 1955, where Nasser enjoyed equal status with Nehru and Tito.

Although Nasser's and Egypt's power and prestige received a gratuitous fillip from extraneous events, notably the Suez affair and the Iraq revolution, and an almost equally gratuitous blow from the 1967 war with Israel, Egypt's wider international ambitions would in any case have become difficult to sustain as the decolonization process ran its course in the 1960s. New independent states emerged, like Algeria and Nigeria, with equivalent potential and priorities of their own, while the economic power of the oil states far outstripped that of Egypt. At the same time, Egypt had drifted farther and farther away from non-alignment into almost total dependence – economic, military and political – on the Soviet Union. It nevertheless managed to maintain a degree of political dominance within the Arab world, through the gruelling years of the 'war of attrition' between 1967 and 1973, probably because even in defeat it was seen as the Arabs' main defence against further Israeli encroachment.

President Sadat restored Egypt's international standing, and the nation's self-respect, by his expulsion of the Russians in 1972 and the launching of the 'October War' in 1973, only to alienate most of his fellow-Arabs by his journey to Jerusalem in November 1977 and the subsequent peace treaty with Israel. President Mubarak has brought Egypt back into a more balanced posture internationally, and gone far towards healing the breach with the other Arab states while continuing to respect the peace treaty. But Egypt is still a long way from recapturing the position of influence it enjoyed under both Nasser and Sadat.

The main questions addressed in this chapter are (a) to what extent Egypt under Mubarak (or any successor regime) can still play a significant role on the world or the regional stage; (b) whether the pro-Western alignment adopted 15 years ago is likely to undergo radical change in the foreseeable future. For convenience, they are discussed under the separate headings of Egypt's relations with (i) Israel, (ii) the Arabs, (iii) Africa, (iv) the United States, (v) Europe, and (vi) the Soviet Union, followed by a passage of – necessarily speculative – conclusions.

Israel

The language of the peace treaty between Egypt and Israel, negotiated at Camp David in September 1978 and finally signed in March 1979, conceals an asymmetry as well as an ambiguity in the attitudes of the two parties that hampers rational discussion of their mutual relationship as well as of the wider Arab-Israeli problem. Sadat's immediate objective was to recover Sinai, and by eliminating the risk of further wars to free Egypt's resources for economic development. Thus did he justify his initiative for domestic consumption. He was no less sincere in his pursuit of a comprehensive Arab-Israeli settlement, with redress for the Palestinians, which became the subject of the other agreement reached at Camp David, entitled 'Framework for Peace in the Middle East'; but he acknowledged that this was essentially a matter for negotiation among all the parties concerned.

For its part, Israel's overriding interest was in neutralizing the most powerful of the Arab forces ranged against it, by means of treaty undertakings backed up by physical guarantees (the demilitarization of Sinai, early warning systems, an international peace-keeping force, etc). The non-military, so-called 'normalization', provisions of the peace treaty were of psychological rather than practical importance, the symbol of Israel's final acceptance by a neighbouring Arab state.

As for the 'Framework for Peace' agreement, the contradictory attitudes of the parties were plain from the outset. To Prime Minister Begin it was a formula providing for a measure of local autonomy for Palestinians living in the occupied territories of the West Bank and Gaza, which would remain permanently under Israeli control. To Sadat (and the United States) it was a transitional arrangement, pending a final settlement of the Palestinian problem which would involve at least some Israeli withdrawal.

The ambivalence on each side, amounting almost to self-deception about its own and the other's true interests and objectives, largely accounts for the sterile and acrimonious state of Egyptian-Israeli relations during the first seven years of formal peace. Israel has accused Egypt of failing to honour the (bilateral) letter of the treaty and Egypt has charged Israel with violating its (multilateral) spirit, above all by the invasion of Lebanon in 1982. In Egypt the invasion was seen as a repudiation of Israel's commitment to a comprehensive peace, intended to highlight Egypt's impotence to help its fellow-Arabs. The government contained its indignation at the time, but four months later felt compelled to react strongly to the Sabra and Chatila massacres – by withdrawing the Egyptian ambassador from Tel Aviv and freezing normalization measures.

When the Likud governments of Begin and his successor Shamir (who had actually voted against the Camp David agreements) gave place in 1984 to the current coalition, the Egyptians had relatively high hopes of Prime Minister Peres. They had been at pains, through direct contacts and visits, to cultivate the Israeli Labour Pary while in opposition, as well as disaffected Likud moderates like Weizmann. They were therefore all the more disappointed that Peres should have found himself compelled by the more pressing issues of Lebanon and the domestic economy to defer serious negotiations with Egypt until the last days of his premiership. Latterly Mubarak for his part, facing American pressure to make the first move, felt obliged for his own domestic reasons to place increasing emphasis on Egypt's single bilateral grievance against Israel, namely the dispute over the strip of beach at Taba that Israel had retained after the final withdrawal from Sinai in 1982. When agreement was finally reached on arbitration, in September 1986, clearing the way for Mubarak's first and only 'summit' meeting with an Israeli prime minister, and for the reappointment of an Egyptian ambassador in Tel Aviv, there was no time left for the pursuit of wider issues. In the event, and despite Peres's assent to the idea of an international conference, there seemed little foundation beyond mere hope for his and Mubarak's joint declaration of 1987 as a 'year of negotiations for peace'.

Nevertheless Egypt's commitment to the search for a comprehensive peace is not in doubt. It is sufficiently attested to by the persistent efforts the regime has deployed since 1979, undeterred by successive disappointments and setbacks – the stagnation of the autonomy talks between 1979 and 1982, the defeat of Carter, the Israeli invasion of Lebanon, Israel's rejection of the Reagan Plan of September 1982, and the failure since 1984 of efforts to construct a negotiating coalition between Jordan, Egypt and the PLO. Egypt itself can perhaps be held responsible for at least one missed opportunity, when Sadat rejected an American proposal in 1979 to promote a Security Council resolution recognizing the political rights of the Palestinians. His motive was probably a personal unwillingness to be associated in such an initiative with the other Arabs, who had just declared their boycott of Egypt, but with hindsight it may be seen as a regrettable mistake. Sadat's successor wisely abandoned the assumption that it was enough for Egypt to lead the way and the others would, eventually, follow, and has taken more pains to coopt negotiating partners.

Mubarak's perseverance is grounded as much in national self-interest as in regional ambition, particularly in the belief that a serious revival of the peace process would strengthen the forces of moderation in the Middle East, and that continuing stalemate will be exploited by extremists whose aim is revolution. It would also, the Egyptians hope, open the door to renewed economic assistance, from the Arab states as well as the United States. Above all, the search for peace, the leitmotif of Egyptian foreign policy for 17 years, has – notwithstanding a suppressed sense of despair as one obstacle succeeds another – become a matter of national pride which no Egyptian government could abandon without calling into question its competence to handle the equally challenging problems at home.

But Egypt has been obliged to recognize that it is no longer in control of the process, and that movement depends primarily on others. Hence the persistent Egyptian endeavour to draw Yassir Arafat and the Palestine Liberation Organization into negotiations even after King Hussein had broken off contact with them. Hence also Mubarak's belated espousal of King Hussein's call for an international conference, which he had previously criticized as futile in view of American and Israeli opposition. Hence, finally, Mubarak's refusal to be discouraged by the failure of Peres as foreign minister to push the international conference idea through the Israeli cabinet, and his acceptance of a subsequent meeting with Peres at Geneva in July 1987.

Even if the time came when all parties were obliged to admit that the peace process was at an end, there would remain powerful constraints against any action by Egypt which amounted to a repudiation of its Camp David commitments to Israel and the United States. These are, in brief, the vulnerability of Sinai to reoccupation by Israel and the risk of the withdrawal of the US civil and military aid on which Egypt largely depends. These constraints are likely to be decisive for both Mubarak and any legitimate successor regime, except in the face of severe provocation, e.g. an Israeli attack on Jordan. Even so, they would have to assume that Israel would have anticipated an Egyptian reaction and be prepared for hostilities in Sinai.

The Arabs
Sadat never forgave the Arab regimes which at the Baghdad summit of 1979 reacted collectively to Camp David by breaking off relations with Egypt and suspending it from the Arab League. But he did not share the discomfort felt by most of his ministers at Egypt's isolation. Far from looking for a rapprochement, he sought to emulate Nasser by appealing to the Arab peoples over the heads of their rulers. In his last year, however, he allowed Egypt's self-interest to prevail to the extent of resuming relations with the Sudan, which had briefly fallen in with the majority Arab line, and embarking on what became a massive (and profitable) flow of arms to Iraq.

Mubarak since the day of his accession has chosen to follow what is undoubtedly the national mood, as well as self-interest, in quietly cultivating the 'moderate' Arab regimes, while avoiding the appearance of running after them. The PLO has been a constant object of these efforts, partly as the key to a revival of the peace process and partly in order to prevent its falling under the control of rejectionist Syria. Indeed, following Syria's expulsion of the PLO from Lebanon in 1983, Egypt became Arafat's staunchest supporter, undeterred by his continual tergiversations. Although Mubarak was eventually provoked into breaking off relations with the PLO in response to the hostile resolutions passed at the Algiers conference of the Palestine National Council in April 1987, he appears to have recognized that this could jeopardize Egypt's standing in the peace process, and efforts to resume contact with Arafat are under way.

Meanwhile most of the Arab states have re-established channels of communication with Cairo, although only Jordan and Somalia have resumed full diplomatic relations. The Egyptians have been disappointed by the failure of others, especially Iraq, to follow suit, which they attribute largely to the equivocal attitude adopted by Saudi Arabia. They tend to discount the official Saudi line that the Baghdad decisions can only be rescinded by a further Arab summit, and to interpret Saudi motives as a combination of fear of provoking Syria and jealousy of Egypt as a potential rival. But even five years ago there was sufficient inter-Arab consensus for Egypt to be elected to the Arab/African seat on the UN Security Council. And, irrespective of the state of intergovernmental relations, the migration of millions of Egyptians in recent years to work in the Arab oil-producing states will have created within Egypt a wider and deeper sense of Arab comity (although there has been friction too) than ever existed before at the popular level.

The political process took a major step forward with Mubarak's attendance in January 1987 at the summit meeting in Kuwait of the Organization of the Islamic Conference, to which Egypt was readmitted in 1984. In calling for a new start in relations between Egypt and its Arab brethren (albeit with a perfunctory condemnation of Camp David) the conference implicitly acknowledged the handicap that the ostracism of Egypt had imposed on the Arabs in their conflict with Israel on the one hand and Iran on the other. Mubarak's subsequent visit to other Gulf states, together with the resumption of substantial economic aid to Egypt by Saudi Arabia and Kuwait, constituted effective proof that the Baghdad boycott decisions had been tacitly revoked. Iraq itself, after seven years of war with Iran, is no longer in a position to pursue the ideas of regional ascendancy which it presumably entertained at the time, nor to resist the claims of others.

As relations with Saudi Arabia improve, one or two others among the moderate Arab governments may feel able to follow the example of Jordan. It seems unlikely however that the formal reconciliation between Egypt and the Arabs, whether through its readmission to the Arab League or a general resumption of diplomatic relations, can be taken much further except in the context of a major advance (or setback) on one or other of the main issues. Although few Arab governments still demand as a price the abrogation of the peace treaty with Israel, and there is no disposition in Egypt to pay it, the presence in Cairo of an Israeli ambassador will remain for many of them a formidable deterrent.

One exception might be the convening of an international conference on Palestine, including Syria. Another might be a major Iranian military success in the Gulf war threatening Kuwait, which brought about the dispatch to its aid of an Arab emergency force including Egyptian units. In any event, thanks to Mubarak's success in Kuwait, Egypt is now well placed, irrespective of the state of formal relations, to consolidate its standing and influence in the Arab world. It might even find scope for playing a mediatory role in some of the numerous secondary disputes with which the region is plagued.

Granted all the shortcomings of Camp David, it may be that Sadat's most enduring legacy is to have established almost unanimous acceptance among both Arabs and Israelis of the principle that a settlement of the Palestine problem should be sought through negotiation. And as the idea of an international conference gains ground there is likely to be increasing recognition among the Arabs that Egypt's unique experience of negotiating with Israel is a major asset to the Arab side, supported as it is by the formidable professionalism and drive of the Egyptian diplomatic machine.

Africa
Although the Islamic Conference, with its large non-Arab majority, has proved a convenient vehicle for Egypt's re-entry into an important part of the international community, it is too large and disparate to be capable of being employed as an effective instrument for political purposes, as Nasser envisaged, whether by Egypt or by any other member. Similarly Nasser's 'African circle' ceased to offer the opportunities he identified for Egyptian leadership once most of the former colonies attained their independence and the numerous offices of national liberation movements based in Cairo closed their doors. Among his more dramatic interventions had been the dispatch of Egyptian troops to the Congo in 1960 and the breaking of diplomatic relations with Britain in 1965 over Rhodesia. Thereafter

Egypt became preoccupied nearer home with the 1967 war with Israel and its aftermath.

Although neither of Nasser's successors showed a comparable interest in southern Africa, their ministers maintained a continuous level of activity within the Organization of African Unity (OAU), which eventually enabled Mubarak to take up the Egyptian seat at African summit meetings. He gave the keynote speech at Addis Ababa in July 1986, and was a candidate for the presidency in 1987 before withdrawing in favour of President Kaunda. Egyptian ministers have also contrived, with the help of successive French governments, to reinforce Egypt's claim to a regional African role by their attendance at the regular meetings of the Heads of francophone African states. The choice of Cairo as the venue for the 1987 annual meeting of the African Development Bank is the latest acknowledgment of Egypt's return to centre stage.

For much of this period Egypt had found itself on the defensive within the OAU against Qaddhafi's campaign to secure its isolation in Africa as well as the Arab world, although latterly Egypt has gained increasing support from those non-Arab African states that feel no antagonism towards Israel. Accordingly Egypt lent ready cooperation, in the form of transit and other facilities, to any third party seeking to check Libyan expansionism, and in particular to French operations in support of Hissein Habre in Chad.

So far, however, Mubarak has resisted the temptation, possibly even American encouragement, to settle the bilateral feud with Libya by direct action. Given Libya's nominal military strength, at least in equipment, its links with the Soviet bloc, and notwithstanding its recent defeat in Chad, Mubarak will have every reason to continue to do so, unless subjected to severe provocation or if an external distraction from domestic problems seems desirable. If, on the other hand, Qaddhafi were to be overthrown by an internal coup, there could be a revival of interest in the experiment of the early 1970s in some form of association between the two countries, although the economic advantages are no longer so evident and the concept has probably been discredited by Qaddhafi's most recent ventures in political union.

Egypt's prime concern in Africa has traditionally been the Sudan, chiefly on account of the Nile waters it controls but also because of its strategic position bordering on so many sensitive areas – Ethiopia, Uganda, Chad and Libya. Sadat's picture of an Egypt menaced by a Soviet-controlled arc of hostile states from South Yemen to Libya may have been overdrawn for American consumption, but the potential threat remains a legitimate source of concern for Egyptian defence planners. They are more immediately concerned about the continuing rebellion in southern Sudan and the strength of Islamic fundamentalism in the north, with the accompanying risk of internal instability and external interference.

During the abortive experiment in political union in Nimeiri's latter period, Egypt reaffirmed its existing defence commitment to the Sudan with clear reference to Libya, and backed it up in 1982 with a modest air defence contingent in Khartoum. At the same time the government recognized that large-scale assistance on the ground was ruled out by logistic difficulties, let alone popular Sudanese sensitivity to Egyptian intervention. Egyptian sensitivities were aroused in turn when the new Sudanese government sought a rapprochement with Libya following the overthrow of Nimeiri in 1985. But the estrangement seems to have been satisfactorily resolved when the Sudanese President and Prime Minister paid visits to Cairo in early 1987.

In the economic sphere there has been much talk of the scope for Egyptian human and technological investment in the Sudan's huge agricultural potential, but again the financial, practical and political difficulties seem insurmountable. Indeed, the traffic tends to be in the other direction – of labour from Nubia to Egyptian industry. The one common problem above all that demands more urgent attention than it has yet received is that of the Nile waters. Egypt is already using more than its allotted share under the existing agreement, thanks to underutilization by the other riparian states. And its rapid population growth is increasing demand to a point which will shortly exceed all existing sources of supply, including Lake Nasser, already depleted by drought to almost its minimum level.

Thus it has become a vital imperative to resume work – at present halted by the rebellion – on the Jonglei canal in southern Sudan, which will both increase the flow to Egypt and yield vast new areas of cultivable land in the Sudan. Mubarak has made periodic attempts to mediate between Sudan and Ethiopia, the country on which the rebels largely depend for supplies and sanctuary, and in 1987 he persuaded President Mengistu to pay his first official visit to Cairo. But Egypt has few cards to play, and it appears that the two governments prefer to conduct negotiations – such as they are – direct.

The United States

As many commentators have noted, the remarkable consistency that the US has shown over the past 40 years in defining its interests and priorities in the Middle East – prevention of Soviet penetration, access to oil, the security of Israel – has been matched by an equally remarkable inconsistency in the policies through which these objectives have been pursued. The inconsistencies and contradictions have nowhere been more evident than in US policy towards Egypt, which has frequently been at the centre of debate. The chronicle is familiar: the cold-war preoccupation with the Soviet threat gave place intermittently to attempts to show understanding for Egyptian and Arab concerns – at the time of the Egyptian revolution, of the aid offer for the Aswan Dam, of US withdrawal from the Baghdad Pact project, during the Suez crisis, and in the early Kennedy period.

But all these efforts came quickly to grief, owing partly to Israeli opposition and partly to Egypt's own actions, such as the Czech arms deal of 1955, Nasser's recognition of China in 1956, his intervention in the Yemen in 1962, and the 1967 war with Israel. The cumulative suspicions and antagonisms thus engendered in effect brought about the wider confrontation that the US feared, with the Soviet Union cast as champion of Egypt and the Arab cause, and the US, deprived of diplomatic relations with Egypt, Syria and Iraq, relying increasingly on Israel in the Mediterranean, and in the Gulf on the Shah.

It is necessary to recall this background when considering whether Sadat's spectacular reversal of alliances in 1972–3 is likely to prove enduring or might be reversed in turn. There was no doubting the enthusiasm and relief with which the Egyptian people greeted Sadat's visit to Jerusalem, and the subsequent peace treaty with its promise of no more wars and economic prosperity. And there has been due recognition, if not gratitude, at both government and popular level, for the massive flow of US aid on which Egypt has come to depend since 1979, although most Egyptians consider it no more than an appropriate recompense for enabling Carter to achieve the one outstanding foreign policy success of his presidency. But there was always a minority of Egyptians, mostly leftists and

Nasserists, who criticized Sadat's swing towards the US as excessive, and a greater number – including two foreign ministers – who opposed Camp David as a separate peace and a betrayal of the Palestinian cause. These views have gained currency and strength over the past seven years through an accumulation of grievances against the US and as the benefits of the US connection have come to be taken for granted.

Sadat probably dreamed of building a special relationship with the US equal to or surpassing that between the US and Israel, but the basis and justification of it had always to be a comprehensive settlement of the Palestine question. Washington's failure, in the face of Israeli intransigence, to deliver any progress towards that goal in some three years of negotiation, put Sadat in an increasingly embarrassing position vis-à-vis his domestic critics. Although opposition to Camp David was only one among several causes of the unrest that preceded Sadat's assassination in October 1981, it was the principal charge he levelled against his critics in the massive security purge which prompted the assassins to act. The motive behind his purge, paradoxically, was to give the lie to foreign speculation about instability in Egypt, which he may have feared the Israelis would use as a pretext for delaying their final withdrawal from Sinai, due in six months' time.

Although the Israelis did withdraw on time, their invasion of Lebanon immediately afterwards (allegedly with American connivance) was a devastating blow to Egypt's pride, and left what is probably a permanent scar on its relations with the US. On top of that, the Reagan Administration's reversion, under the impact of Afghanistan and the Gulf war, to the global approach to the Middle East (the 'strategic consensus'), the pressure from Washington for military facilities in Egypt, the 1983 agreement on strategic cooperation with Israel, the failure to follow up the Reagan Plan of September 1982 after the collapse of its policy in Lebanon, the forcing down of the Egyptian aircraft carrying the *Achille Lauro* hijackers, and finally the Irangate revelations, have created a growing feeling of disenchantment with the US and the conviction that Washington's policies are now almost exclusively determined by Israeli interests with little regard for Egypt.

Many Egyptian politicians also suspect that the US, in addition to its declared policy of maintaining Israel's military superiority over the Arab states collectively, shares the Israeli preference for a continuing division between Egypt and the others, in particular Saudi Arabia. And the government complains openly about the administration of the US aid programme in Egypt compared with the treatment Israel receives: the heavy interest charges levied on loans for military supplies (which were running at some $700 million a year before the US agreement in mid-1987 to negotiate interest relief), the rigid and cumbersome restrictions on the disbursement of civil aid, and the numbers of American advisers in the country.

These are common enough reactions to aid programmes in almost any country, and they are compounded in Egypt by memories of its former dependence on other foreign advisers, both British and Russian. Nor are the Egyptians entirely without fault. The US could complain in turn about their failure to make adequate provision for interest payments, about the obstacles that the bureaucracy continually creates in the way of efficient aid administration, and more generally about the lack of political realism in the claim to receive equal treatment with Israel. Nevertheless the sense of helpless dependence on a foreign patron lends itself to nationalist exploitation, and there have been several periods when anti-American feeling has been widespread and intense in Egypt, of which Mubarak has been obliged to take account. He has accordingly taken a series of steps to dilute Sadat's total identification of Egyptian with US policies – his public appeal to Reagan to open a dialogue with the PLO, his refusal to grant the US unfettered access to military facilities on the Red Sea, his resumption of ambassadorial relations with Moscow, his resistance to American pressure for unrequited concessions to Peres, and – most recently – his failure so far in 1987 to make his customary annual visit to Washington.

Given the relatively unsympathetic reaction of Washington to these moves, and the current unpopularity of the Reagan Administration in the Arab world, it seems probable that the pressures on Mubarak to make further gestures of independence of the US will grow, in the absence of a major shift in Administration policy in favour of Egypt and the Arab side on either Palestine or the Gulf war. The external pressures, from Syria, Libya and the newly reunified PLO, can probably be contained, especially in the light of Egypt's improved standing since the Kuwait summit, unless the US were to give further offence by some action, such as cancelling an offer of arms or mounting an abortive anti-terrorist operation, which evoked a united Arab response.

Internal pressures, on the other hand, may come to exert a greater effect on Egyptian foreign policy in the immediate future, although they are not easy to assess. Traditionally the average Egyptian is less concerned about foreign affairs than most other Arabs, and foreign policy scarcely featured as an issue in the elections to the People's Assembly in April 1987. However, two political groupings which have dissentient views on foreign policy, the Nasserists and the communists, remain debarred from political activity. The election manifesto of the Muslim Brotherhood included a call for a review of Egypt's special relationship with the US, and since the Brotherhood emerged as the principal opposition party it might have been expected to press this proposal in the Assembly in addition to its principal demand – for exclusively Islamic legislation. The fact that it has not yet done so could be due to embarrassment at the abortive terrorist attack on American diplomats that took place in May 1987, and which the opposition parties were quick to condemn.

Europe
The deterioration in Egypt's relations with the US is likely to encourage Mubarak to try to strengthen the links with Europe which he has been at pains to cultivate since he came to power, and which were largely neglected by Sadat. Egypt's initial anxiety about its exclusion from the Euro-Arab dialogue following Camp David proved unfounded, since the dialogue itself ran into the sands. But Egypt has been more assiduous than most other Arab governments in addressing the European Community collectively about its chief political concerns, a practice which has advantages for both sides, especially in multinational fora where the EC functions as a group. Mubarak's successful efforts to persuade the major EC countries to contribute contingents to the Multinational Force in Sinai also reflected his desire to avoid appearing exclusively dependent on American arms, which in addition might have been misrepresented as the controversial Rapid Deployment Force in disguise.

The Egyptians have no illusions about the EC's capacity to influence Washington to adopt a more active and favourable policy on the central political issue of the Middle East, and have not seriously attempted to invoke it since 1982, when a so-called Franco-Egyptian initiative at the United Nations was blocked by the threat of an American veto. But they have welcomed the declaratory pronouncements that the EC has made from time to time, most recently in support of the idea of an international conference. In the separate field of disarmament, the Egyptian government sees further scope for cooperation with Europe in promoting its proposal for a nuclear-free zone in the Mediterranean.

There is perhaps a greater mutuality of interest and scope for collaboration in the economic sphere. Like other Mediterranean Arab countries, Egypt enjoys various preferential arrangements with the EC under the Mashraq agreements, and is the second largest recipient worldwide of EC food aid. In the field of trade there is much at stake, for the EC countries collectively are both Egypt's largest export market and its most important supplier, although there is an incipient conflict of interest over agricultural products with the EC's new Mediterranean members. Provided this can be overcome, the European market could be of critical importance to Egypt's efforts to revive its agriculture as the engine of economic recovery.

There is, in fact, a greater degree of genuine interdependence in the relationship between Egypt and Europe, grounded in genera-tions of economic, cultural and social intercourse, than in the relationship between Egypt and the United States. Although the latter overshadows the former, owing to Egypt's massive dependence on US economic and military aid, it is essentially a one-way relationship – of client to (distant) patron, recipient to donor – not yet 10 years old and with no intrinsic guarantee of permanence. The reciprocal nature of the European connection, by contrast, rests not only on the facts of geography and history but – for better or worse – on Europe's greater vulnerability to Middle East events. At present, unfortunately, while EC governments prefer to conduct their relations with Egypt individually, with an eye to competitive national advantage, the potential of the collective relationship seems likely to remain unrealized. The agreement reached with the 'Paris Club' in May 1987 on rescheduling Egypt's massive external debt could perhaps pave the way for a more collaborative approach to future trade.

The Soviet Union
The breach between Egypt and the Soviet Union, precipitated by

Sadat's expulsion in 1972 of thousands of Soviet advisers, and widened by his abrogation of their treaty of friendship in 1976, is perhaps the most serious and long-lasting reverse that Moscow has suffered at the hands of a Third World country. Since Sadat's original action was prompted not so much by any offence on the part of the Russians (other than a general resentment of their obtrusive presence in Egypt) as by a desire to engage the support of the US, his policy was and remained impervious to any conciliatory moves from the other side.

Neither was it affected by the occasional gestures that an American administration chose to make to Moscow for its own purposes, e.g. the enlistment of Soviet observers in the United Nations Truce Supervision Organization after the 1973 war (Egypt denied them permission to enter Sinai) or the Soviet-American joint declaration of October 1977 aimed at reviving the Geneva Conference (which was overtaken by Sadat's visit to Jerusalem). Indeed it was part of Sadat's stock-in-trade to play up the communist threat at home and abroad in order to keep American support for Egypt up to the mark, most notably when he expelled the Soviet ambassador in the context of his purge of alleged subversives in the month before his assassination. He had earlier cancelled the reappointment of an Egyptian ambassador to Moscow (in abeyance for several years) in protest against the Soviet invasion of Afghanistan, and made a point of publicizing Egypt's material assistance to the Afghan resistance.

Mubarak and his Minister of Defence, Field Marshal Abu Ghazala, fully share Sadat's suspicions of the Soviet Union, largely as a result of their direct experience of Soviet society and policies during their military careers. Mubarak made his views plain soon after he became president, and did not include the Russians among those alienated by Sadat to whom he made early gestures of conciliation. The fact that he delayed the resumption of ambassadorial relations until late 1984 suggested that he saw no political advantage in such a move to outweigh the risk of adverse reactions in Washington. As noted above, Egypt also held out almost to the last before subscribing to the consensus in favour of an international conference, long the Soviet panacea for the Arab-Israeli problem – with its corollary of a Soviet seat at the table. Egyptian suspicions may well have been revived by the role the Soviet Union played in 1987 in bringing together the opposing factions of the PLO at the

Palestine National Council conference in Algiers, which in Egyptian eyes purchased unity at the cost of hard-line resolutions hostile to Egypt.

Thus the Soviet Union faces an uphill task in attempting to regain its former influence in Egypt, in spite of the openings offered by American mistakes and omissions. During the Sadat period the Russians showed remarkable forbearance under provocation, and avoided supporting their more extreme Arab clients in calling for the overthrow of Sadat or the abrogation of the Camp David agreements. In Mubarak's presidency, too, they have refrained from forcing the pace, although under Gorbachev inertia has given place to more calculated and positive policies towards the Middle East in general, while US policy remains in disarray.

Meanwhile both sides have preferred to concentrate in their bilateral dealings on practical matters of mutual interest. The first step was the return in 1982, without publicity, of a small number of the Soviet technicians expelled by Sadat whose services were indispensable to the operation of three Soviet-built industrial plants, the steel mills at Helwan, the aluminium smelter at Nag Hammadi and the Aswan Dam. Subsequent negotiations have revolved, for at least the past two years, around the major question of Egypt's long outstanding military debt to the Soviet Union, amounting to some $3 billion, payments on which were suspended by Sadat. These finally culminated in March 1987 in a comprehensive economic agreement, providing for the rescheduling of the debt over 25 years, with all interest waived, as well as for new arrangements to promote bilateral trade, including a more realistic Egyptian exchange rate, and further Soviet participation in industrial projects.

It is a reasonable presumption that Moscow will have been anxious to point a contrast between its readiness to reach a compromise and the deadlock between Egypt and the United States over military debts of broadly similar magnitude. On the Egyptian side, one may also postulate an element of reinsurance and a desire to remind the US that Egypt is not to be taken for granted. But there is little sign in Egypt of a positive interest, at either government or popular level, in a return to the former close relationship with the Soviet Union. In addition to previous bitter experience, the special ties between the Soviet Union and Syria are a particular constraint on both sides against pushing a rapprochement too rapidly or too far.

Conclusions

While Egypt aspires to a global, 'non-aligned', foreign policy, and has the breadth of experience and talent to sustain it, the interaction of external events and domestic opinion since the death of Sadat has caused the regime to give priority to the Arab world. Most politically conscious Egyptians still consider Egypt the natural leader of the Arabs, and look back with nostalgia to the periods of ascendancy it enjoyed under both Nasser and Sadat. Yet in neither period was this ascendancy complete. The 'reactionary' regimes which Nasser hoped to overthrow survived to become Egypt's equal partners, and indeed financiers, in the aftermath of the 1973 war, perhaps the highest point that Arab solidarity has ever reached.

Since that solidarity foundered on Camp David, and the Camp David 'framework for peace' foundered in turn on the Israeli invasion of Lebanon, Egypt has taken the line that the creation of an Arab consensus is a prerequisite for any further progress on the central problem of Palestine. The aim is no longer overall hegemony, merely to recover something of Egypt's former influence in the Arab family via a place at the negotiating table, where Egypt has undoubtedly a contribution to make. The convening of an international conference would represent the optimum outcome for this policy, irrespective of whether it produced concrete results. Meanwhile there is little sign of serious pressure, either domestic or external, to renege on the peace treaty with Israel, since no one wishes to court the probable consequences of a further round of war and a major breach with the United States. Equally, there is little enthusiasm for further advances in 'normalization', except in so far as such gestures may help Peres to promote his peace policy.

On the other hand, Egypt's special relationship with the US is coming under increasing strain, now that the US has manifestly abandoned its commitment to 'full partnership' with Egypt in the peace process, if not all pretence of an active role. The Administration would appear to have no greater concern for Egypt than that the country should remain stable and friendly, while the Congress appears to judge Egypt's value chiefly by its responsiveness to the requirements of Israel. In these circumstances the regime as well as the public may be increasingly tempted to question the general assumption that the annual $2.2 billion appropriation of US aid is indispensable to Egypt's survival, especially since a substantial proportion of the cumulative total of civil aid has not yet been disbursed. There will at least be a growing tendency to reinsure with alternative sources of aid, whether Arab, European or Soviet. The policy of cautious disengagement from Egypt's exceptionally close political ties with the US is likely to continue in parallel, though with little risk of an actual reversal of Egypt's essentially pro-Western alignment, unless the US were to make excessive demands of Egypt as the price of its support. As Egypt continues to strengthen its relations with Europe and the Soviet Union, the result should be a healthier posture, more in keeping with the regional balance of power.

The chances of a major change in Egypt's international alignment would, naturally, be greater if Egypt were to undergo an internal upheaval. The seriousness of the change would depend on the nature of the upheaval. Various hypothetical developments are postulated in preceding chapters, most of them involving a deterioration in the economy leading to popular unrest and rioting on the pattern of January 1977, an outcome which successive Egyptian governments have invoked as an argument against radical economic reform. If the government were able to control the situation only by resorting to severe repression, it would risk forfeiting support in the West, at least temporarily. If the government proved unable to suppress the disorder completely, one possible result might be an uneasy coalition of military and religious leaders (assuming that Muslim extremists were behind the uprising), calling itself revolutionary. In view of the presumed economic origins of the crisis, any revolutionary regime would be likely to seek to reduce its dependence on (and indebtedness to) the US. But since no such regime is likely to have communist leanings, there would be little pressure for a complete reversal of alliances. A revolutionary Egypt probably could not even afford, because of its acute economic straits, to emulate Iran in adopting an attitude of equal hostility to both superpowers, and might be obliged to continue in a modified form of alignment with the West.

On the other hand, the reaction against the American connection would inevitably put Camp David under strain, and in such a tense situation an Israeli government might well decide to make either precautionary or pre-emptive moves in Sinai. There would be a high risk of escalation in mutual threats, and this could lead to the unravelling of the peace treaty. The military consequences would depend on whether Egypt went further and demanded the withdrawal of the Multinational Force and Observers (MFO) from Sinai. Since to do so would be to invite an Israeli attack, there is a presumption that Egypt would not, remembering the lesson of 1967. But the possibility cannot be ruled out. In any event, the prospect of a negotiated comprehensive peace would recede out of sight.

As to the other regional effects of an internal upheaval, if the armed forces were to take control there would be little significant change. There might be some sabre-rattling in the direction of Israel, both for popular effect and to satisfy those officers who still regard Israel as the main enemy. There would be no greater enthusiasm than there is now for sending troops to help Iraq, though there might be more inclination to use force against Libya if Qaddhafi renewed his challenge in the Western Desert or the Sudan. However, the emergence of a fundamentalist regime in any form would create psychological shock-waves throughout the Middle East similar to the impact of the Iranian revolution.

Although it is hard to imagine a fundamentalist regime in Egypt making common cause with *Shi'a* Iran against Iraq, the effect on morale on both sides in the war would be profound and conceivably decisive. The spectacle of the two most populous states in the region under Islamic governments would also cause acute alarm in Saudi Arabia and the Gulf states, and give heart to their own religious extremists. Even if the new regime occupied itself entirely with domestic affairs and followed a passive foreign policy, it seems inevitable that the relative stability that the Arab world (Lebanon excepted) has enjoyed for some 20 years would be severely shaken.

While the prognosis for any significant improvement in Egypt's economic and social condition is poor, the foregoing analysis suggests that Egypt's potential as a stabilizing force (or the reverse) within the region is so great that the West cannot afford to contemplate either a continuing steep decline, let alone an economic collapse, or Egypt's departure from its present pro-Western alignment. This implies that US and other international aid must be maintained at least at its present level, with a combination of more sensitive direction and steady pressure for measures of economic reform.

In the political sphere it implies that there must be a serious effort by the US to pursue a more even-handed policy as between Egypt and Israel, avoiding unnecessary slights to Egypt, and to revive the search for a comprehensive settlement of the Palestine problem. There is much to be said, too, for attempting to associate the Soviet Union with the overall endeavour, since previous US policy of preventing Soviet involvement for global strategic reasons has proved not only ineffectual but counter-productive.

6
CONCLUSIONS

Lillian Craig Harris*

Egypt has entered a critical period in its search for solutions to domestic problems. Serious social and economic pressures are fed by urban crowding, large-scale unemployment, challenges to traditional society, popular political disillusionment and, some would argue, insufficiently stringent and misdirected government policies. Increasingly, the Egyptian government has had to grapple with popular unhappiness arising from its inability to fulfil its part of the 'social contract' for economic prosperity. Nor can domestic and external affairs be separated: Egypt's foreign and domestic policies interact, just as do the economic, social and political components of internal affairs.

Earlier chapters discuss this interrelationship. Mourad Wahba describes popular anger and loss of respect for the state over the 'domination of foreigners in the national economy as well as the polity', while Michael Weir points out Egypt's resentment over being 'taken for granted' by foreign patrons and predicts 'increasing stress' in the US/Egyptian relationship. Ali Abdallah and Michael Brown, who see no alternative to long-term dependence on external aid, predict that this dependence will 'erode Egypt's long-standing desire to regain a dominant and independent role in regional politics'. Thus, although external assistance has provided relief to the Egyptian economy, such help may yet have a very high price.

Not only is there domestic resentment over foreign dependence (and consequently over real and perceived foreign efforts to intervene in Egypt's internal affairs), but external assistance may have encouraged a dangerous tendency to put off difficult decisions, to delay the day when Egypt is forced to work out its own salvation.

The situation is not unrelentingly sombre, of course. During recent years Egypt has steadily improved its international position, as Michael Weir points out, diversifying its international contacts and seeking a more balanced relationship between East and West. Over the past year several positive developments have also occurred in Egypt's domestic climate, among them increases in revenues from tourism, domestic production and petroleum sales. Agreements with the International Monetary Fund and other lenders have provided a critical breathing-space to the beleaguered Egyptian government. Egypt, it seems, is regarded by the West as too important to be allowed to sink into economic chaos. Almost certainly, therefore, it will continue to have access to significant international funding. But will this be enough?

A negative assessment

The assessments of Egypt's social, political and economic prospects given in the preceding chapters are distressingly negative. Egypt's problems seem to have reached a critical point, at which simply muddling through may no longer be a sufficient response, as Nazih Ayubi points out. To offer a blueprint for what Egypt's response should be is beyond the scope of this small volume, but its authors do show agreement on a number of key issues. Chief among these is that Egypt's economic problems are now acute, that the mid-1987 IMF agreements were palliative only, and that careful reform measures are still urgently required.

Economic reform remains a subject of intense debate within Egypt, a political issue with sufficient power to cause popular unrest and one which places constant pressure on the government – as demonstrated, for example, in November 1986, when Ali Lutfi was replaced as prime minister by Atef Sidqi, another distinguished economist. In extreme circumstances, economic issues could even endanger the regime itself. The Egyptian government knows that serious economic reform is needed, but fears that attempts at radical surgery could cause the patient to rise up and smite the surgeon.

Conclusions

Most economic reforms remain unimplemented, therefore, and, in some areas, semi-articulated. The real dilemma which the government faces is how, on the one hand, to acquiesce to economic necessity, including the demands of external creditors, and, on the other, to maintain internal stability, given the growing incapacity of the welfare state.

The observation in earlier chapters that Egypt needs more assertive leadership (or, as Wahba phrases it, 'a sense of direction') is frequently made both in Egypt and abroad. It is indeed difficult to argue that Egypt would not benefit from more decisive, more far-sighted economic policies. Yet President Mubarak's task is neither easy nor enviable and, given the potentially explosive issues with which the government must deal, a degree of caution in his policies is certainly understandable. Moreover, although he has moved neither quickly nor decisively to address Egypt's economic dilemmas, the country's continuing political stability is by no means the least of his achievements.

No immediate danger of upheaval

Despite growing popular dissatisfaction with living standards and the increased popularity of groups which advocate radical, even violent, religious solutions to the country's problems, there does not appear to be an immediate danger of unmanageable civil unrest. Riots by security police in early 1986, and religiously inspired assassination attempts during 1987, have not shaken the government's claim that it can control the activities of extremists, whether politically, economically or religiously motivated. Liberalization of the law to allow the Muslim Brotherhood to be represented in parliament has been broadly criticized as a dangerous government mistake which will provide an opportunity for extremists. But although the situation bears watching, there is no evidence, for the short term at least, that the government cannot continue to cope effectively with violent dissent. On balance, tentative, if incomplete, steps towards a broader democratic base have provided a valuable political pressure-valve.

Earlier chapters indicate that there is no imminent danger of a radical change in the Egyptian political system. Even during times of crisis, such as the 1967 defeat by Israel, Nasser's death in 1970 and Sadat's assassination in 1981, the Egyptian system has demonstrated great powers of continuity. For administrative, economic, social-structural and religious reasons, an Iranian-style revolution seems unlikely in Egypt. A widespread desire for internal stability, frequently expressed as fear of political upheaval, makes it even more unlikely that the Egyptians will totally reject their present system – whether they describe it as 'nascent democracy' or as 'limited dictatorship'. Nor, in the short term, is there likely to be a radical change in Egypt's international political orientation. Formidable constraints exist on any repudiation of Egypt's Camp David commitments or on a return to alignment with the Soviet Union, as Michael Weir observes.

It is important for outsiders to realize that religious revivalism in Egypt and its most obvious manifestation, the resumption of traditional dress, does not necessarily indicate a commitment to religiously motivated political violence.[1] The proliferation of outward signs of religious commitment may often indicate, instead, a need among the people to reaffirm their identity through a return to threatened traditional values. Yet this situation, too, bears watching, for true believers everywhere are among those most easily persuaded to try radical solutions. The political climate, moreover, remains fraught with potential trouble as Egypt struggles with the concept of establishing a loyal opposition in the face of elements which advocate radical change and violent solutions.

If the standard of living continues to deteriorate, and unless tensions can be relieved by greater political participation, there must be a point at which domestic disappointment and dissatisfaction will result in serious political backlash. The trend of the foregoing analysis suggests that a crisis point does exist, though it is difficult if not impossible to know how much pressure people can take, or over what issue violence is most likely to be triggered. In the past, however, violence has resulted from an outraged sense of justice (the 1977 bread riots and the 1986 police riots) and, in the case of foreign pressures, a wounded sense of national honour (the response to the American interception of an Egyptian aircraft following the *Achille Lauro* incident).

What is evident is that the considerable achievements of the Mubarak years risk being overwhelmed by the immensity of the dilemmas which remain. Much of the internal criticism of the Mubarak era arises from the frustrations of those who desire more decisive policies to end Egypt's economic distress, and of those – a vocal and expanding minority – who demand a greater voice in Egypt's search for prosperity, tranquillity and social justice. These two areas will demand the attention of successive Egyptian governments over the coming years. The risks at stake are immense, and simply to avoid failure will be an enormous achievement.

Obstacles to reform
Paradoxically, however, political passivity, rather than violent activism, seems to pose the greater immediate threat to Egypt's political future. As Ayubi and Wahba both point out, social and economic problems have engendered feelings of powerlessness among the people so that, although Egyptians are far from indifferent to political developments, their lack of confidence in their ability to change conditions breeds both hopelessness and cynicism. Such passivity may assist the government in maintaining internal security, but it is highly unfortunate for Egypt's political life in general. For example, owing to a widespread, and not altogether incorrect, belief that the outcome is predetermined, a majority of Egyptians do not even bother to vote in national elections.

As Ayubi points out, Egyptians suffer from a paucity of viable political choices. Although opposition parties present 'an alternative domain of concern over morality, ethics and family life', they fail to provide the ordinary citizen with practical solutions to his daily problems, much less to national dilemmas. This is what gives the militant Islamic groups their opportunity: they are able to offer to those who see no human solution to life's problems the option of starting anew according to God's will. But, in practice, opposition policies remain largely irrelevant to solving Egypt's problems. The Wafd position that more democracy is necessary is sound – but incomplete. The Islamic radicals' pressure for the application of *shari'a* is itself a divisive tactic which often contains concepts hostile to modern development and international ties. The socialists, too, appear to believe that a solution lies in their being put into office, though what their subsequent policies might be is not clear.

Workable programmes are not, of course, a prerequisite either for successful election or for successful revolution. But in Egypt even solid political alternatives are difficult to identify. The government's opponents remain surprisingly unorganized, are usually unable to cooperate, and have yet to coopt any specific 'cause' as a rallying point. Nor do any of the opposition groups – fortunately in some cases – offer a nationally acceptable and charismatic leader. No Atatürk, Khomeini or Corazon Aquino has emerged. With various trumpets all giving uncertain sounds, most Egyptians simply retreat.

Up to now, government concern has been to placate popular dissatisfaction with its own performance rather than to encourage more than token participation in the political process. The pre-eminence of the National Democratic Party will only be endangered if the balance of cynicism tips (possibly as a result of a serious deterioration in the standard of living) towards government and away from the NDP's would-be rivals. In such an event, large numbers of Egyptians could be expected to become more politically active – but possibly more violently than constructively.

The effect of popular political apathy on yet another group may not at first appear so evident. Earlier chapters discuss the importance of the Egyptian military, a bureaucracy unto itself, whose most important mission is to safeguard the regime. Having done away with the monarchy in 1952, the Egyptian military has since then functioned, usually behind the scenes, as a powerful key to internal stability as well as to Egypt's political leadership. No aspirant to public office, whether opponent or supporter of the regime, can afford to antagonize the military. It can never be forgotten, moreover, that the military would certainly be tempted to use its powers of coercion if the political process moved against its wishes. This could have both positive and negative applications, depending on one's political viewpoint. But the continued prominence of the military in political affairs represents a potential danger to the democratic development of Egypt's political system.

The apparent lack of will on the part of both government and people to carry out reforms is a serious impediment to economic change. If the Egyptian government were actually to apply the fundamental reforms which it promised the IMF that it would implement as the condition for recent agreements, it would have first to conduct an intense preparation of popular opinion for the coming national belt-tightening. Such preparation is not evident. Nor, if it were, could people be expected to respond enthusiastically in view of the past failure of government promises. Instead, the government's economic reliance on foreign countries and foreign organizations strengthens the Egyptians' widely held perception that, at least to some degree, their country remains a victim of outside forces which seek to keep it politically and economically weak and its government dependent. Widespread perception of governmental weakness arouses public anger, further impeding the government's ability to implement economic reforms and strengthening the hand of those who advocate radical change.

For most of its modern history, Egypt has been under the control of non-Egyptians, and it is understandable that the concept of exploitation plays an important role in the Egyptian view of history. But it would be an error to assume that there is 'an Egyptian viewpoint' on external culpability for Egypt's dilemmas or, indeed, on any of the problems discussed in the preceding chapers. Differences of viewpoint and opinion between Egyptians and outsiders mirror similar differences within Egyptian society itself. Misunderstanding and lack of communication between Egyptian political, social and economic groups are probably deeper than most outsiders, and possibly even most Egyptians, realize. This disunity and lack of communication is yet another major impediment to systemic reform. The genuine surprise expressed by the National Democratic Party over the good showing of the Islamic opposition in the April 1987 parliamentary elections indicates a lack of awareness on the part of the ruling party, and perhaps even an insensitivity to the economic plight and political aspirations of others, that could broaden divisions within Egyptian society during the coming years.

An even more evident threat to national reform measures is religious sectarianism. Pressures for the implementation of *shari'a* augment the divisions in Egyptian society, and the proponents of radical religious politics can be expected to use social disunity as a foil for their strident challenge to the government, a challenge which will in coming days tax the government's security responses. Moreover, not only does extremism flourish in some sectors of the Muslim body politic, but (what is cause and what effect?) Coptic Christian groups have in the last decade become more militant. There are those who now see a further deterioration in the Copts' access to mainstream Egyptian economic and political life.[2] The truth or falsehood of this claim may not be as significant as a growing belief among Copts that they have cause for fear.

Yet another impediment to reform or even to carrying out present policies, lies in the inefficient and outsized government bureaucracy, described by Abdallah and Brown as 'combining delay and corruption in equal measures'. A laudable undertaking begun during the

Nasser era to ensure employment for all has swollen the bureaucracy and resulted in gross underemployment for millions – with consequent mismanagement, stalling, red tape, wastage and inefficiency. Radical reorganization is urgently needed. But the bureaucracy is unlikely to participate willingly in an exercise which would result in demotion, deprivation of privilege and even unemployment for thousands of its members, with a consequent dangerous rise in social and political tensions. The government faces a most difficult problem in its efforts to break what the Chinese call 'the iron rice-bowl' – the bureaucratic sinecure.

The greatest long-term obstacle
Ultimately, however, it may not be economic problems, social divisions or militant religious politics which constitute the most serious obstacle to Egypt's future stability and prosperity. Although earlier chapters provide no consensus on this point, it would appear that the problem which underpins all others is Egypt's virtually unchecked population growth. The impact of the population explosion is still felt mainly in urban areas, but it is a phenomenon which has already put immense pressures on the economy, on social services and on political decision-making – as Abdallah and Brown agree. Development, the democratic process, international influence and even national 'honour' are all in some measure held up or held hostage by the effects of population growth. Abdallah and Brown are also correct in saying that a large population does provide certain economic advantages. But the assertion that 'the sheer size of Egypt's population can be viewed as an asset in the long term' does not appear to follow. Nor does Wahba's conclusion that 'the high rate of population growth is a serious problem only because of its emotiveness as an issue and because of congestion in the towns' seem entirely warranted. However, his point that 'a radical reappraisal of the economic and social reasons for population growth is ... vital before an appropriate and effective strategy can be devised to deal with it' is manifestly correct.

Egypt is a country of limited usable land and limited resources which now imports over 50% of its food and, with an already extremely high rate of unemployment, is required to create 450,000 new jobs a year just to keep that unemployment rate from rising. At the current population growth rate (2.8% per year), there will be 70 million Egyptians by the year 2000, a phenomenon referred to by President Mubarak as 'a dreadful increase in population'.[3] Over the next decade, crowding will intensify in Egypt's already congested schools, with inevitable rises in illiteracy. The overloaded social services system could break down completely. Living standards can be expected to continue to deteriorate, accompanied by a reduction in employment opportunities for the disadvantaged, including the poor who seek better lives for their children and women who have found a foothold on the ladder to individual choice through economic freedom. Even if draconian birth-control measures were taken immediately, the pressures of an expanding population would continue to influence all spheres of Egyptian public and private life well into the next century.

Most Muslims do not object to birth control on doctrinal grounds, but contraception is regarded by many conservative Egyptians, Copts as well as Muslims, as an attack on the family, the main support of Egyptian life. In recent years the issue has also been politicized by certain religious leaders who claim that birth control is actually a scheme designed by non-believers to limit the number of Muslims. Thus, opposition to family planning has become for some a religious duty. As Wahba points out, the government's inadequate presentation of family planning programmes has also retarded acceptance of the need to restrict family size.

The apparent belief of many Egyptians that labour export and industrialization can solve Egypt's surplus labour problems is dangerously erroneous. Labour migration is no longer even the temporary solution that it was in the 1970s. Opportunities for labour migration have peaked and will almost certainly continue to shrink in coming years. Instead of providing foreign remittances, thousands of returning workers will raise social tensions by joining, with heightened expectations, the domestic labour market. Industrialization can absorb some surplus labour and even relieve local unemployment pressures. But the obstacles to creating an industrialized economy are formidable: the source of the massive funding which would be required for widespread industrialization has yet to be identified, as does even the appropriate industrial structure for Egypt's needs.

Nor does the possibility of expansion into the desert as a response to population pressures offer more than limited hope. Desert lands can be used for certain types of industry and, on a small scale, even for housing; but environmental, ecological and economic constraints sharply restrict their use. It is doubtful that large numbers of people would, without coercion, leave the Nile Valley for the desert. As for agriculture, according to figures published by the US Agency for International Development, approximately $10,000 per year over a seven-year period are required to bring one acre of the Western Desert successfully under cultivation[4] – to say nothing of subsequent problems of salinity, climate and water resources.

Limited water resources alone negate the hope that the desert will prove to be a vast unexploited arena for housing, industrial or agricultural expansion – and underscore the need to curtail population growth. Egypt remains totally dependent on the waters of the Nile and the only major project likely to increase its water resources is the Jonglei Canal scheme in southern Sudan, work on which has been halted by civil war. Should the canal be finished, it would add only marginally to Egypt's water supply. Meanwhile, the African drought – now in its eighth year – has left Lake Nasser dangerously low. Even if the drought ends, development projects and a rapidly growing population are placing unprecedented demands on limited water resources.[5] Stark choices between electricity and irrigation could feature in the not too distant future.

What can be done?
Egypt is in difficult straits, its future course threatened by economic chaos, popular dissatisfaction and a growing radical opposition. The avoidance of shipwreck through massive borrowing has been achieved, to at least some degree, at the expense of Egypt's political independence and has, consequently, increased the divisions in Egyptian society. As Professor John Waterbury observes, 'It may be that because of its geopolitical importance Egypt can live indefinitely on external largesse ... But corporate containment, public subsidies, and inefficient state capitalism cannot be expected to paper over the stark realities of limited resources and a growing population.'[6] Previous chapters indicate that change must come, though whether it will be managed or convulsive remains unknown.

Several conclusions emerge:

(a) Serious economic reform will be delayed at Egypt's peril. According to Abdallah and Brown, if undesirable developments, including economic decay and domestic political unrest, are to be avoided, 'Egypt will have to take fundamental action now'. The hour is so late, in fact, that even immediate action cannot save Egypt from continuing economic crisis over the next several years.

(b) Effective population-control programmes are clearly necessary. According to one observer, 'The fact that this issue touches Muslim sensibilites has pushed the debate onto the ideological level and limited serious public discussion. But the severity of the problem is such that this contrived silence cannot be allowed to last.'[7]

(c) Popular alienation from government and political lethargy are as much a legacy of past experience as a reflection of the failings of the present government. Nonetheless, despite measures in recent years to move towards a pluralistic political system, the democratic process has not been guaranteed. Unless this situation changes, there is little hope for a non-violent future: the many who opt out will become prey to the few who espouse radical change – or pawns for the military, which will step in to restore order. As Ayubi notes, 'the only way of preventing the hard economic situation from leading to a political explosion is to involve people more closely in the problems, and in the process of *trying* to solve them'.

At present, lack of efficient means of political participation encourages young people in the direction of the radical religious movements, as Ayubi also points out. Expansion of the political power-base is, therefore, a necessary ingredient in attempts to address social and economic grievances. Though the pace of reform remains controversial, everyone pays at least lip-service to the concept that people need to be brought into a more participatory and positive partnership in the democratic process. Time alone will pass final judgment on the effectiveness and wisdom of President Mubarak's policy of providing 'dosages of democracy in proportion to our ability to absorb them'.[8]

Obviously the government cannot be held entirely responsible for the political development of its rivals. But it remains unclear how much blame for the present lack of political choice should be ascribed to government failure to provide an opportunity for democracy to develop, and how much to the immaturity of the political opposition. Will the political opposition make constructive use of greater democracy? Will a more open political system merely expand political access for those who advocate violent means to power? Is violence really the only alternative to apathy? Or will growing political activism by the radical fringe help to jolt the majority of Egyptians, who are neither political nor religious extremists, out of their political lethargy?

(d) Unless it is itself reformed, the government bureaucracy will almost certainly prevent implementation of the range of other critically needed changes. As Abdallah and Brown note, inefficiency, waste, lack of coordination, redundancy and corruption are the hallmarks of the Egyptian bureaucracy. (Most of these adjectives apply as well to the commercial elites which curry favour with the bureaucracy.) There is little hope that a massively overmanned bureaucracy with 46 economic authorities and 372 public-sector companies, supervised by 18 different ministries, can carry out any policy effectively, let alone develop effective economic policies to convey the state towards industrialization and modernization.

(e) If Egypt is to overcome its present dilemmas, its friends will need to resist the temptation to take unfair advantage of the leverage over Egyptian economic and political life which external patronage and financial dependence provide. The Egyptian/US relationship, in particular, appears to be heading towards dangerous shoals as a result of miscalculated American policies and the Egyptian backlash against foreign dominance. Michael Weir describes 'a growing feeling of disenchantment with the United States, and the conviction that Washington's policies are now almost exclusively determined by Israeli interest, with little regard for Egypt'. Egyptian resentment over external attempts at manipulation and lack of consideration for domestic sensitivities have been inadequately grasped by American policy-makers and political institutions. An Egyptian official recently summed up Egyptian frustration by telling his State Department interlocutors that, in the Egyptian-American-Israeli triangle, 'Egypt knows who is the wife and who the mistress. But even the mistress has her rights.'

It should be clear to all that Egypt's peace treaty with Israel and close relationship with the United States are mixed blessings for the Mubarak regime. The failure of popular expectations that peace would allow Egypt to achieve economic recovery, the perception that the treaty has forced Egypt into a position of subservience to the US, and Israeli policies and actions towards the other Arabs provide convenient whips which the opposition uses to flail the government. American efforts to force the Egyptians away from a 'cold peace' and into greater friendliness with Israel have increased tensions between Egypt and the US as well as between Mubarak and his opponents. Foreign insensitivity to internal Egyptian political currents (as more than one earlier chapter observes) undermines the domestic authority of the Egyptian government. On the other hand, it is also evident that until the Egyptian bureaucracy reveals itself to be more competent and less corrupt, irksome foreign controls on aid funds will continue – as will carping and wounded pride over lack of trust on the part of patrons.

If the future is to be characterized by a chain reaction of Egyptian responses to American 'arrogance' and American responses to Egyptian 'ingratitudes,' neither regional peace nor Egyptian stability will be served. What is as yet insufficiently understood by American policy-makers is that the US 'needs' Egypt as much as the US 'needs' peace in the Middle East. There are other sources of friendship, and perhaps even of money, for Egypt. But there is only one Arab country which has made peace with Israel; only one state which incorporates 40% of the Arabs; only one country on the crossroads between Africa, Asia and Europe.

Unfortunately, the thrust of US policy appears geared towards using Egypt rather than towards understanding how Egypt, as a trusted friend, can strengthen itself. The United States must recognize Egypt's need to strike a balance between East and West, its unique position in the Arab world, the constraints of national pride and the limits to Egypt's ability to improve its relationship with Israel. The Egyptians are painfully aware that no European government can influence Israel so much as the United States can – when it wants to do so. But there is room for a more forceful European role as interpreter, and even broker, of the Egyptian position to the United States. Egypt's international policy under President Mubarak remains very much in the interest of the West, and both American and European policy-makers would do well to seek ways to alleviate tensions while encouraging the Egyptians to stay the course.

Egyptian/US tensions could enhance opportunities for Egyptian/ European cooperation. But rather than sit back and enjoy American discomfiture, as some Europeans have done, energies should be devoted to the formulation of more constructive policies. Until now the prevailing view in Europe appears to have been to allow the Americans to foot the bill so that Europe could profit. There is considerably more that the Europeans could do to assist two-way commercial benefits. Michael Weir points out that so long as EC governments 'conduct their relations with Egypt individually, with an eye to competitive national advantage, the potential of the collective relationship seems likely to remain unrealized'.

Moreover, since there appears to be no alternative for the foreseeable future to continued external assistance for Egypt's beleaguered economy, the Europeans need to reassess their role in what is surely an international responsibility to assist regional stability. Concern for Middle Eastern stability has already brought a generous response from states as diverse as Saudi Arabia and Japan. During the 1980s contributions by the Japanese government to the Egyptian economy – including aid for construction, health, food production and agricultural development – have on some occasions been exceeded only by those of the United States. Unless European governments are prepared to be more generous in their aid programmes, the Egyptians will not listen any more carefully to their economic advice or accord them any greater credibility as allies.

In discussing Egypt's problems, or in criticizing Egypt for failure to implement reforms, it is well to remember that situations frequently look quite different from the inside. This may be particularly true for those who, whether constrained by bureaucracy or by compassion, are seeking to edge Egypt towards reform without causing unbearable hardship to the poor. The Egyptians are a resilient people who must in the end make up their own minds how best to bind up the rifts in their society and implement the measures which can begin to heal their economy.

But outsiders will continue to be intensely interested in and closely involved with Egypt's future. For if internal problems were eventually to cause such a key regional player to collapse, the repercussions would extend far beyond the Nile Valley and, indeed, beyond the Middle East. Even a continued state of weakness and prolonged international dependence will have a deleterious effect on peace in the Middle East – as well as extremely negative consequences for the lives of the 50 million Egyptian people.

Notes

1 For lack of a better term 'religious revivalism' is used here to refer to the phenomenon of increased attention to Islam as political and social theory which became noticeable during the early 1970s and

accelerated after the Iranian revolution. The term is not intended as in any way pejorative of Islam itself (I avoid the even more controversial term 'Islamic fundamentalism'), since I see a distinction between true reformism and the radicalism which characterizes certain segments of the present Islamic revival. A balanced discussion incorporating a variety of viewpoints on the conflict between politically oriented Islam and secularism is found in Barbara Freyer Stowasser (ed.), *The Islamic Impulse* (Washington, D.C.: Center for Contemporary Arab Studies, Georgetown University, 1987).

2 See, for example, John King, 'The Fear of Egypt's Copts', *Middle East International*, 25 July 1987 (no. 305), p. 16.

3 BBC, *Summary of World Broadcasts*, Middle East and Africa, 27 April 1987.

4 Quoted in Herman Frederick Eilts, 'Egypt in 1986: Political Disappointments and Economic Dilemmas', *The Washington Quarterly*, April 1987, p. 121.

5 See, for example, 'Water: Fears Over Lean Years', *The Financial Times*, 29 June 1987.

6 John Waterbury, *The Egypt of Nasser and Sadat: The Political Economy of Two Regimes* (Princeton, N.J.: Princeton University Press, 1983), p. 434.

7 Tahseen Basheer, 'Youth Has an Agenda of Change', *International Herald Tribune*, 27 June 1987, p. 10.

8 BBC, *Summary of World Broadcasts*, Middle East and Africa, 14 February 1987.

BIBLIOGRAPHY

Abdel-Khalek, Gouda, and Tignor, Robert. *The Political Economy of Income Distribution in Egypt*. New York and London: Holmes and Meier, 1982.

Atiya, Nayra. *Khul-Khaal: Five Egyptian Women Tell their Stories*. Cairo: American University in Cairo Press, 1984.

Ayubi, Nazih. *Bureaucracy and Politics in Contemporary Egypt*. London: Ithaca Press, 1980. (St Antony's Middle East Monographs, No. 10.)

Aliboni, R., *et al*. *Egypt's Economic Potential*. London: Croom Helm, 1984.

Burns, W. J. *Economic Aid and American Policy Toward Egypt*. Albany, NY: State University of New York Press, 1985.

Cooper, Mark N. *The Transformation of Egypt*. London: Croom Helm, 1982.

Critchfield, Richard. *Shahhat, An Egyptian*. Cairo: American University in Cairo Press, 1982.

Dessouki, Ali Hillal, ed. *Democracy in Egypt*. Cairo: American University in Cairo Press, 1978. (Cairo papers in Social Science series.)

Fahmi, Ismail. *Negotiating for Peace in the Middle East*. London: Croom Helm, 1983.

Hansen, Bent, and Radwan, Samir. *Employment Opportunities and Equity in Egypt*. Geneva: International Labour Office, 1982.

Heikal, Mohamed. *Autumn of Fury: The Assassination of Sadat*. London: André Deutsch, 1983.

Hinnebusch, Raymond A. *Egyptian Politics under Sadat*. Cambridge and New York: Cambridge University Press, 1985.

Hopwood, Derek. *Egypt: Politics and Society, 1945–1984*. London and Boston: Allen and Unwin, 1985.

Bibliography

al-Husseini, Mohaez Mahmoud. *Soviet-Egyptian Relations 1945–85*. London: Macmillan, 1987.

Kamel, Mohammed Ibrahim. *The Camp David Accords: A Testimony*. London: Routledge & Kegan Paul, 1986.

Kepel, Gilles. *The Prophet and Pharaoh: Muslim Extremism in Egypt*. London: Al Saqi Books, 1985.

Kedourie, Elie, and Haim, Sylvia G., eds. *Modern Egypt: Studies in Politics and Society*. London: Frank Cass, 1980.

Kelley, Allen C., Khalifa, Atef M., and El-Khorazaty, M. Nabil. *Population and Development in Rural Egypt*. Durham, NC: Duke University Press, 1982. (Studies in Social and Economic Demography Series, No. 5.)

Kerr, M.H., and Yassin, E.S., eds. *Rich and Poor States in the Middle East: Egypt and the New Arab Order*. Boulder, CO: Westview Press, 1982.

Mabro, Robert. *The Egyptian Economy, 1952–1972*. Oxford: Clarendon Press, 1974.

MacDermott, Anthony. *Egypt After Nasser*. London: Croom Helm, 1987.

Nyrop, Richard F., ed. *Egypt: A Country Study*. Washington, DC: American University and US Government Printing Office, 1983.

Quandt, William B. *Camp David*. Washington DC: Brookings Institution, 1985.

Riad, Mahmoud. *The Struggle for Peace in the Middle East*. London: Quartet, 1981.

Rugh, Andrea B. *Family in Contemporary Egypt*. Cairo: The American University in Cairo Press, 1985.

Saunders, Harold. *The Other Walls*. Washington DC: American Enterprise Institute for Public Policy Research, 1985.

Vatikiotis, P.J. *The History of Egypt*, 3rd edn. Baltimore, MD: The Johns Hopkins University Press, 1986.

Vatikiotis, P.J. *Nasser and His Generation*. London: Croom Helm, 1978.

Waterbury, John. *The Egypt of Nasser and Sadat: The Political Economy of Two Regimes*. Princeton, NJ: Princeton University Press, 1983.

Waterbury, John. *Hydropolitics of the Nile Valley*. Syracuse, NY: Syracuse University Press, 1979.

Wilkan, Unni. *Life among the poor in Cairo* (trans. Ann Henning). London: Tavistock, 1980.

Related titles

Turkey and the West
David Barchard

Turkey is strategically important to the West, yet set apart by its geographical location, political system and level of economic development. Turkey's political and economic situation, its foreign policy and all aspects of its relations with the Western world are examined in this paper. The author concludes by assessing the likely costs and benefits of closer Turkish relations with the West, and reviewing the ways in which those relations might evolve.

The Third Oil Shock
edited by Joan Pearce

Twice in recent years OPEC has agreed on a large increase in the official selling price of oil, with adverse consequences for the world economy. In March 1983, for the first time in its history, OPEC decided collectively to reduce prices. What are the implications for the world economy of a period of lower oil prices? This Special Paper presents expert analyses of the main issues. An overview paper assesses the gains, costs and dilemmas generated by lower oil prices. Other essays consider the effects on oil-exporting countries, developing countries, Eastern Europe, the international financial system, OPEC, energy insecurity and the oil industry.

Developing Country Debt
H. A. Holley

The external indebtedness of the developing countries and the inadequacy of current flows of development finance have given rise to a set of problems that seem likely to persist in one form or another for the rest of this decade and beyond. This study focuses on the role of the commercial banks as suppliers of funds to the most heavily indebted countries; the reasons for their involvement; the lengthy process of debt rescheduling; the implications for the soundness of national banking systems; and the likely future of international bank lending under the Baker initiative. It also considers the role of official lenders, both bilateral and multilateral, the consequences of the fall in oil prices and other changes in the world economic environment, and the reaction of debtor countries to a prolonged period of adjustment and austerity.

ROUTLEDGE & KEGAN PAUL